MW01119309

FASTING SECRETS REVEALED

Breakthrough Fasting

Charles A. Rhodus

Charles A. Rhodus
FASTING SECRETS REVEALED | Breakthrough
Fasting © 2020 Charles A. Rhodus

https://www.charlesarhodus.com

https://www.amazon.com

All rights reserved. Duplication of material in
this book is not permitted, without prior
permission from the author. All Scriptures
are from the King James Version unless
otherwise noted. Edited by Charles A.
Rhodus Printed in the United States of
America.

I dedicate this book to my loving wife Tammy. She has been committed to prayer and fasting with me from day one.

Table of Contents

1 / SECRETS OF THE STRONGEST DRIVES OF THE BODY

My head is pounding, feels like a thousand migraines. Why did I come this way? My feet keep slipping on the gravel on this slope. It is so hot. It must be at least 110 degrees. My legs feel like rubber. I cannot go any further right now.

These voices in my head are nonstop. I cannot get away from them. I guess I have been out here for at least thirty days at this point. My stomach feels like it has turned inside out, and I am so thirsty. I must find some water. I ran out a couple of days ago. I keep chasing these mirages. When I get to the top of this slope, maybe I can see a pool or a spring of water.

That is an idea. I could make these stones into bread. I am so weak I can hardly go. I could just eat a little and then restart the fast tomorrow. I know it would help this pain in my head. No, no, I cannot do that.

Man shall not live by bread alone, but by every word that proceeds out of the mouth of God.

As I lay here in this sand, I feel like I am literally at the temple in Jerusalem, at the top corner on the pinnacle. I can see the entire city from here. Why should I cast myself down? I know the angels are always protecting me. No Satan, I will not do that. Thou shalt not tempt the LORD thy God.

Finally, a pool of water. I will just lay here for a while and sip. The sun is going down. The heat today has been brutal. There is no shade out here. I will stay here tonight by the pool. These voices do not stop. I can hardly sleep. The dreams, the nightmares. The sounds at night with the darkness and torment in my head is unbearable.

I must be going. The sun is up. It looks like today may be cloudy, and the wind is causing a sandstorm. I can hardly see. I must cover my face. I need to find a safe place until the wind dies down. Maybe the clefts in the rocks over there will be some shelter for a while.

Now that the wind is dying down, I need to climb this mountain. Why am I doing this? Something is driving me, pushing me upward. My heart is pounding out of my chest. My energy levels have picked up. This climb will take days, but it is like I cannot refrain. I must get to the top.

What a view. It is so clear at the top. I feel successful. I feel powerful. I can do anything. I feel that the world is at my fingertips. From here I can see the nations. I have a view even to conquer the kingdoms of the world. They will all bow to me. Worship Satan? No. I will not worship anyone but the LORD God. No, I will not bow to anyone but He. I have not come to conquer the nations. I have not come to rule the world but to give my life as a ransom for all. Oh, the pressure. I can hardly stand this. I am so dizzy, weak, and hungry.

Something has lifted from me like a thousand pounds has been removed from my shoulders. I felt a release, a pressure that is gone, my mind is clear. So thankful for these angels that have come. I am stronger now. I feel so much better. I can make it now.

Luke 4:14 And Jesus returned in the power of the Spirit into Galilee: and there went out a fame of him through all the region roundabout.

Jesus was the greatest fasting and prayer warrior that has or ever will live. Jesus the man, was the greatest example of discipline, holiness, prayer and fasting. The Bible does not give us every account of his praying and his fasting. There is no need for that because we know that the Gospels are an overview of the life of Jesus. The Gospels are the writings of four Godly men from different vantage points.

Luke 4:2 Being forty days tempted of the devil. And in those days he did eat nothing: and when they were ended, he afterward hungered.

Heb 4:15 For we have not an high priest which cannot be touched with the feeling of our infirmities; but was in all points tempted like as we are, yet without sin.

Matt 4:2 And when he had fasted forty days and forty nights, he was afterward an hungred.

We know from the scriptures that the 40 days in the wilderness was a time of great temptation. Satan came to Jesus to tempt him, hoping he would fall and destroy the plan of redemption. Note the passage says that Jesus "did eat nothing". It does not say that he went without water. Jesus fasted as a natural man to feel the sufferings of temptation and, feel the pain of doing without food. Medical science teaches us that a healthy person can go several days without water before he harms his health. Now, after the 40 days of fasting, Jesus became hungry. He went back into the cities and the Bible teaches us here that he became famous. I do not believe that Jesus had a goal to be famous so to speak and, nor should we? He became famous because of the miracles that happened through him.
The strongest drive in the human body is to eat, to sustain itself. Jesus conquered the greatest desire and the greatest need of the human anatomy. He conquered the drive to eat. When a man or woman can conquer his

drive to eat, he can curb any appetite or conquer any addiction of the human body. The second greatest desire of human flesh is that of procreation, more commonly known as sex. The 3rd greatest need for humanity after eating and sex is that of fellowship. Now there are exceptions to the rule, but for most people, this would be the order they would come in. Now let me go back to number three again so you understand what I mean. The need for fellowship/friendship is important to most of us. There are people out there that would rather be alone most of the time. There are exceptions to the rule. Let me further prove my point about these three top needs of the human body. If you were in a desert, a scorching desert for days, what would you want the most? Would you want to #1 eat, including a drink #2 procreate or #3 hang out with some friends and talk? Your greatest need would be to sustain yourself with food and water and stop the growl of that ole stomach. Well we know why it is true, without water, again you will die, and no one likes to be hungry. It stops that flesh in its tracks and for a person seeking after God, he can more readily pursue Heavenly things. The things of the Spirit of God become more prominent and important to him or her. People rarely go without food unless they are dieting or are on some carnal fast to prove a point.

We are fasting not to lose weight but to gain insight and to seek the face of almighty God. It is the serious believer that will push back the plate, and say, "the heavenly things are more important than things of this world".

Many years ago, a pastor told a story of how he asked his church to join him on a fast for several days. There was a farmer in the church that came to him afterward, and complained how difficult it would be for him, because he worked a physical job. The farmer reluctantly began the fast with the rest of the church body. He called the pastor several times each day, complaining about how miserable he was. The pastor told him before the week was over, he would hurt all over. On one evening of this fast, they were having church, and a mother brought her baby daughter for prayer. She had a growth on her neck that was serious. The growth was to be removed by surgery, but the church prayed. Nothing seemed to happen at that moment when they prayed, but they continued to believe God for a miracle. The next night they were having another church service, and the mother noticed that the growth on her child's neck had shrunk . She called the pastor and informed him of the wonderful news. He told her "I will see you at church and, I believe that by the time you get here the growth will be gone". The growth was not gone, but it was small. It was so small that with her finger she could touch it and roll it around under the child's skin. That night the growth disappeared. God had done an amazing miracle through this fast of the church body. The farmer came to the pastor and apologized and, said "pastor, I'm with you, I will fast with you anytime. Call upon me anytime to fast whenever there is a need"

Jesus is the greatest example for every Christian. The scripture records one fast of 40 days, but there could have been many. No doubt there are other shorter fasts that he did. Jesus is the perfect example in every way, to lead us unto holiness and consecration. The Lord Jesus was not a politician, and neither was he a comedian of any sort. He had his face set and his heart fixed on what he came for. He could not have accomplished the miracles without the noble sacrifice of a life of fasting. He had a mission to accomplish. He was winning souls every day. His days were filled with teaching and doing miracles. As we read, thousands followed him to hear his words. What Jesus did in 33 years on this earth could not be written, the scripture says, in all the books of the world.

John 21:25 And there are also many other things which Jesus did, the which, if they should be written every one, I suppose that even the world itself could not contain the books that should be written. Amen.

The flesh will hinder all the goodness of God, the power of God, and the gifts of the Spirit. When a person desires God enough, he will push back the plate. The old flesh nature reveals to us, it is time to seek God by prayer and fasting.

Fasting and prayer opens the door to new dimensions. The initial receiving of the Holy Ghost is not a stopping point. It is the beginning of new dimensions. You will never have greater dimensions after your new birth without seeking them. This is where fasting and prayer come in. It can launch you into new spiritual arenas of miracles, the power of God, and the gifts of the Spirit.

Fasting is what will take you deeper. You will stay in an immature walk with God. It is like a baby that was born that stays a baby. He never walks, runs, talks, or works a job. If you want to get over the difficulties of the spiritual rollercoasters, consistent fasting will conquer that.

You will be limited in doing the will of God unless, the flesh is defeated. It must be under subjection to the Spirit. You must decide. Your body wants to comfort and pampering. When you fast, your body is being starved, not only of food, but also of carnality.

In the next chapter, I will discuss the mustard seed. Most believers have been taught wrong. It is said, that with a little faith, the "size" of a mustard seed, you can move mountains. We examine that in the next chapter and show you the error in that teaching.

2 / SECRETS OF MUSTARD SEED FAITH

In this next passage, we see a very desperate situation with a father and son. We do not know the boy's age, but if he was 6 or 16, he was at his end. The father is desperate, even crying out and begging for help for his possessed son. The passage tells us in a few words that the boy would run to the water and to the fire to hurt himself. How many times did he run to the open sea or run to the Jordan River to jump in to drown himself? Did he run toward open flames to burn himself? Did he have a spirit of suicide or was he so delusional that he did not know what he was doing? The scripture says he was vexed, deaf, and dumb. Not only was he deaf and dumb, but Jesus said he had a spirit of deafness and dumbness. In today's medical world, no doubt he would have had a diagnosis with one of the popular names. Every type of sickness and disease nowadays has a diagnosis and a name. Many of these conditions are demonic spirits, as showed by Jesus in the passage.

Matt 17:12-21 But I say unto you, That Elias is come already, and they knew him not, but have done unto him whatsoever they listed. Likewise shall also the Son of man suffer of them.

13 Then the disciples understood that he spake unto them of John the Baptist. 14 And when they were come to the multitude, there came to him a certain man, kneeling down to him, and saying,

15 Lord, have mercy on my son: for he is lunatick, and sore vexed: for ofttimes he falleth into the fire, and oft into the water.

16 And I brought him to thy disciples, and they could not cure him.

17 Then Jesus answered and said, O faithless and perverse generation, how long shall I be with you? how long shall I suffer you? bring him hither to me.

18 And Jesus rebuked the devil; and he departed out of him: and the child was cured from that very hour.

19 Then came the disciples to Jesus apart, and said, Why could not we cast him out?

20 And Jesus said unto them, Because of your unbelief: for verily I say unto you, If ye have faith as a grain of mustard seed, ye shall say unto this mountain, Remove hence to yonder place; and it shall remove; and nothing shall be impossible unto you.

21 Howbeit this kind goeth not out but by prayer and fasting.

Mark 9:25-27 When Jesus saw that the people came running together, he rebuked the foul spirit, saying unto him, Thou dumb and deaf spirit, I charge thee, come out of him, and enter no more into him.

26 And the spirit cried, and rent him sore, and came out of him: and he was as one dead; insomuch that many said, He is dead.

27 But Jesus took him by the hand, and lifted him up; and he arose.

Extreme situations need extreme measures. The disciples of Jesus could not help the boy because of their small faith. They did not have fasting faith because, they were not fasting. Jesus said that we need faith as a grain of mustard seed. Look at the word "as". Remember that little word because we will focus on that for a few minutes. Why could not the disciples free this boy? They were trained and taught by Jesus. They saw by example how he healed and delivered people, but they could not deliver this boy. They could have easily walked away and said, "it must not be the will of God for him to be delivered". Jesus walked into the situation and turn things around. He had a lot of fasting in the shadows, thus He could move in faith for any situation.

We must carefully look at this passage. Many teach that the small size of the mustard seed is all the faith you need. If this is the case, then what was the problem with the disciples? Do you not think they had at least a little faith? How could they spend so much time with the master and, not have at least a little faith? So, if they had a little bit of faith, then why could they not deliver this boy? They had a little faith, but a little bit will not move mountains or pluck up trees or do miracles of this sort. It is not the small faith that can get this done. It is a big faith. It is a strong faith. This is the difference between Jesus and the disciples. He had fasting faith, and they had faith without fasting. Do you the reader have a little faith? Do you have faith the SIZE of a mustard seed? If you do, no doubt you are casting devils out of people all the time. No doubt you are raising the dead, opening blind eyes, and many great miracles. I am being facetious here. A little faith does NOT get the job done. Many Christians have never seen a miracle, but still they say, "we need only a little faith to see mountains moved".

So, what is the passage saying? If it is not talking about small faith moving mountains, then what in the world is it saying? So again, look at the word "as". "if you have faith as a grain ". The word "as" has nothing to do with the SIZE of a mustard seed. It is referring to the CHARACTER of a mustard seed. Now someone can argue that Jesus was talking about the size of a mustard seed because he mentions the size of a mustard seed in Mark 4:30,31.

Mark 4:30-31 And he said, Whereunto shall we liken the

kingdom of God? or with what comparison shall we compare it?
31 It is like a grain of mustard seed, which, when it is sown in the earth, is less than all the seeds that be in the earth:

By rightly dividing the Word we can see that, in this passage Jesus was not talking about miracles, nor was he talking about faith. He was talking about the Kingdom. Mark chapter 4 has nothing to do with Matthew chapter 17. They are two completely different subjects, conversations, and teachings. It is not a good policy to put passages together just because they have similar wordings. It is always worth looking at but, looking at the context of each passage we see they are two different subjects.

Now let me highlight Matthew chapter 17 verse twentyone. "Howbeit this kind goeth not out but by prayer and fasting". You and I both know people that died before their time. We both know people that have serious health conditions right now. We see the babies suffering from unique health conditions like cancer, but our little faith does not get them healed and delivered. If it is just a little faith that we need, why are they still suffering? Why have the people we have loved died before their time? I said earlier that the disciples were not fasting, so thus they could not deliver the boy. We know this because in another place Jesus told us they were not fasting.

Matt 9:15 And Jesus said unto them, Can the children of the bridechamber mourn, as long as the bridegroom is with them? but the days will come, when the bridegroom shall be taken from them, and then shall they fast.

So now we know for sure that the disciples were not fasting. They did not have fasting faith. They had little faith like the size of a mustard seed, but they did not have faith "as" a mustard seed. There is a difference. The word "as" is referring to the character of. The character of the mustard seed. What is the character of a mustard seed? Many years ago, I heard preaching about the mustard seed. The preacher would make statements like the mustard seed is a seed of endurance. The mustard seed can endure a flood, we could run it over by a bulldozer and come back and still grow. The sun cannot scorch it, and the floods cannot drown it. Yes, the mustard seed is extraordinarily strong. It is not just known for its strength and endurance but also its growth.

In the year 1857, a man by the name of Francis Bacon wrote about the mustard seed. From what I could see, his writings had nothing to do with religion or faith. He wrote about how the mustard seed could endure the cold and how it had its own heat. How it comes back yearly and not die like other seeds. He also called it a "strong" seed. Barnes notes say, though the seed is exceedingly small, it constantly grows to the largest herb on earth. So, a true mustard seed will grow large results. Clarke's commentary says it refers to the greatest degree of faith. (This cannot be true if it is referencing the size, because Jesus rebuked small faith.) Five times in the gospels Jesus rebuked small faith. If small faith can move mountains, pluck up trees, and deliver demon-possessed boys that are deaf and dumb, then why did Jesus rebuke the demon? The truth is, small faith cannot do these things, and Jesus was not referring to the "size" of faith in Matthew chapter 17. He was referring to the character of faith. Here is one verse on small faith for your reading.

Matt 8:26 And he saith unto them, Why are ye fearful, O ye of little faith? Then he arose, and rebuked the winds and the sea; and there was a great calm.

No, it is not the tiny faith that gets the blessing. It is enduring, powerful faith that grows and stretches, that can endure the flood, the fire, and the storm. Faith that will believe in the face of opposition. Faith that will pray again and again and again and keep believing and speaking. We as Holy Ghost filled people have the power, but we do not have the faith many times. It is not a power problem, but a faith problem. I used to believe that we had the power of God by some measure. Through much study of the word, I do not believe that any longer. I believe that all God's power of creation is inside of us to do any kind of miracle that is needed.

Do you remember the story of Elijah, how he called down fire and destroyed those men that approached him? There was a second group that approached him, and he called down fire and killed them, a third group, and they died. God spoke to him and said "stop". Stop killing these guys, listen to them. Elijah had the power of God and he knew his authority. What he had with all of that, was faith. Faith to speak the Word. Faith to call the miracle. Elijah was a man of fasting and he had fasting faith. What about the story of Joshua when he was in the heat of battle and spoke to the sun and said "sun, stand thou still"? The universe stood still at the command of Joshua. He spoke to the sun and the moon to stay where they were because he thought they came up and down in the sky. He did not understand the rotation of the planets, so that is why he spoke to the sun and the moon. His lack of scientific knowledge did not hinder his faith. His miracle was bigger than he ever knew. The entire universe came to a halt and, the rotation of the planets stopped for part of a day so Joshua could win a battle. No doubt Joshua was a man of fasting and had fasting faith.

Some people have lowered the requirements to get a remedy for these extreme life problems. They will not be answered, without prayer and fasting. It is a trick of the devil to think we will cast out demons, move mountains, etc. on some little, tiny faith. It is not the little faith that Jesus is looking for, but he is looking for a strong character of faith. Faith "as" a grain of mustard seed. Now understand, I am not saying that you cannot get prayers answered with a little faith. It does not take ten days of fasting to see God do a miracle. It is faith that moves the mountain and not the fast. When the disciples asked Jesus "why could we not deliver him", Jesus told them, "because of your unbelief". They had unbelief because they were not fasting. They were not to fast until the bridegroom was taken away. It is an unbelief problem. Fasting and prayer helps unbelief. Fasting and prayer are what strengthens the faith of an individual. Some people believe easier than others. Some people are natural doubters, but even those individuals can have strong faith and receive a miracle.

The North American culture tries to give us everything for a dime. It is a three-minute car wash, microwave popcorn, and anything else that could be done in a moment. We by nature try to get everything we can for nothing and without paying a price. Powerful faith has a price. Are you willing to pay that price? You will not have that faith, by just attending church. Thank the Lord for the measure of faith, but we need to go from faith to faith and from miracle to miracle.

Rom 12:3 For I say, through the grace given unto me, to every man that is among you, not to think of himself more highly than he ought to think; but to think soberly, according as God hath dealt to every man the measure of faith.

Rom 1:17 For therein is the righteousness of God revealed from faith to faith: as it is written, The just shall live by faith.

So, as it says that every man is dealt a measure of faith which means a limited portion. So even the atheist was born with faith. The Hindu and the Muslim were born with faith. Everyone has that small limited amount of faith. God expects us to hear His Word and grow our faith. God responds to faith like nothing else. The quickest way to have your faith speed up is by hearing "faith" preaching and teaching. Jesus always taught and preached faith. It is faith preaching that produces the miraculous. When we add fasting and prayer to this mix, nothing shall be impossible to you.

Gal 3:2-5 This only would I learn of you, Received ye the Spirit by the works of the law, or by the hearing of faith?
3 Are ye so foolish? having begun in the Spirit, are ye now made perfect by the flesh?
4 Have ye suffered so many things in vain? if it be yet in vain.
5 He therefore that ministereth to you the Spirit, and worketh miracles among you, doeth he it by the works of the law, or by the hearing of faith?

What kind of faith was it that Paul the Apostle spoke to the crippled man, that made him stand up? What kind of faith was it when the shadow of Peter healed the sick? If these miracles were done with small faith, then why do you and I let people walk out of church sick and unsaved. The truth is, miracle faith is not small faith.

Everyone reading this book has at least small faith. If that being true, the demons should be cast out and mountains should move. Some would agree that they have never cast out a demon and or seen the sick healed by their prayer. The flesh is the veil that keeps us from God. When the veil (the flesh) is torn, then we can enter that holy place and see a greater demonstration.

Matt 27:51 And, behold, the veil of the temple was rent in twain from the top to the bottom; and the earth did quake, and the rocks rent;

Heb 10:20 By a new and living way, which he hath consecrated for us, through the veil, that is to say, his flesh;

I want you to have that strong miracle faith. Jesus wants you to have that strong miracle faith. The way we get it is pushing back the plate and seeking his face. We are not seeking power but direction, boldness, faith, and humility. Praying and fasting is more about the relationship than anything. When our old man is dead, we can hear from God. Our flesh is that veil, like the veil of the temple in Matthew chapter 27 that separated the holy place from the most holy place. As Jesus' body was ripped to shreds on the cross, so our flesh needs to be ripped to shreds, so to speak by fasting and prayer. If we die with him, we can live with him. If we humble ourselves, he will exalt us in due time.

The, "easy believeism" and microwave Christianity have deceived millions. There is no bypass, no circumventing of the miraculous, it still takes fasting with prayer. You can get miracles without fasting, and get prayers answered but, as Jesus said, "this kind goeth not out but by prayer and fasting". Some things will not happen without it. It is easy to say, well it must not be the will of God, and let it go. We can miss so many miracles, healings, and deliverances because, we will not push back the plate. We do not want to pray the all-night prayer meetings. Why then expect significant results when we have not given a noble sacrifice. Yes, Jesus paid the great sacrifice, but there is a price to pay for great faith.

A friend called me to pray for his sister at her home, of whom was diagnosed with breast cancer. They gave her six months to live. It seemed like a very hopeless situation. She at one time was a dedicated Christian that was faithful to church and filled with the Holy Ghost. She now was backslid for some years. So, we got to her home and went in the front door and she was sitting in a small chair waiting for us. We had a moment of small talk and we prayed. By the authority of the name of Jesus, we rebuked the spirit and spoke healing into her body. Suddenly, she spoke with tongues. I asked her, when we were done praying, "I noticed you were speaking in tongues, how long has it been since you did that?" She said it had been years. Of course, we left the home not knowing the real outcome of her situation but, hoped and believed for the best. A couple years after meeting with her, my friend called me to testify about her healing. He said she had been back to the doctor and they could not find any trace of cancer. The more wonderful thing about this miracle is, she had no medicine, surgeries, chemotherapy or radiation therapy. The miracle was fully in the hands of God and we give him total praise and glory for her healing. To add to this miracle, several years later, he called me again and said "listen, I want you to know my sister is still healed and not had any trouble or needed any medical treatment". Glory to God!

It is not the small faith that gets things done; it is the faith with the character of a mustard seed. Faith that will hold on, keep on, and be strong in the face of opposition. Fasting faith is the faith that will move mountains, cross oceans, and walk through the flames. Fasting faith is the faith that can raise the dead, open blind eyes, deaf ears, make the crippled walk, and supply any other needed miracle.

The fact is, fasting does not move God. Fasting changes us as individuals. Fasting crucifies the fleshly desires, wherewith allowing the individual to believe in a greater degree. When the flesh is in control of an individual, faith has a hard time reigning. That is why we must fast and pray to "keep under our body and bring it into subjection".

The person who is fasting and praying does not have small faith. He has great faith, or at least faith that is growing. The person who does not pray and fast has small faith. Did Jesus mean in Matthew chapter 17 that we will have small faith if we would fast, or did he mean we would have a strong, powerful faith? You cannot have it both ways. Let us not make this teaching contradictory. It is not the small faith that gets things done; it is the faith with the character of a mustard seed.

You may be familiar with the story of the Seven sons of Sceva in the book of Acts. They tried to cast the devil out of a possessed man, to no avail. The evil spirit jumped on them and they ran away naked and wounded, the Bible says. They tried to cast the devil out in the name of Jesus, of whom Paul preaches. In contrast, look at Paul, how he dealt with the woman with a spirit of divination, and how she was constantly advertising him. He spoke to the evil spirit to come out, and it did. Paul had fasting faith where the sons of Sceva had little faith. The Apostle Paul had faith "AS" a grain of mustard seed, and the seven sons of Sceva had faith the SIZE of a mustard seed.

Acts 19:11-16 And God wrought special miracles by the hands of Paul:

12 So that from his body were brought unto the sick handkerchiefs or aprons, and the diseases departed from them, and the evil spirits went out of them.

13 Then certain of the vagabond Jews, exorcists, took upon them to call over them which had evil spirits the name of the Lord Jesus, saying, We adjure you by Jesus whom Paul preacheth.

14 And there were seven sons of one Sceva, a Jew, and chief of the priests, which did so.

15 And the evil spirit answered and said, Jesus I know, and Paul I know; but who are ye?

16 And the man in whom the evil spirit was leaped on them, and overcame them, and prevailed against them, so that they fled out of that house naked and wounded.

What are we seeking? We are seeking for faith without limitations. Faith that can move any mountain, uproot any tree, heal any disease. Again, it is not the small faith that will move the mountain, etc., it is faith that has the character of endurance, the ability to bounce back, to survive the floods, the scorching heat of the sun, and the pressure that comes through the trials of life. It is faith that believes in the Word of God, regardless of the prognoses or what the natural senses say or feel. This is the character of a grain of mustard seed.

3 / SECRETS OF OVERCOMING THE SINFUL NATURE

God's most beautiful creation, Adam, and Eve. He made every planet and every star. He causes the sun to shine twenty-four hours. He causes the oceans to rise and fall with the tide. He causes the rivers to flow and the waterfalls to fall. He causes the leaves to fall and the seeds to grow. Everything you could imagine that grows has its origin with God. Look at the fetus in the womb. It starts so small and day by day it develops organs, fingernails, etc. and then is born after 9 months. What beauty God has created.

Adam was made from the dust of the ground. Eve was made from his rib. They were made perfect. They were without sin or flaw. There was no sickness, disease, or iniquity, in that beautiful creation of the first two people.

We understand according to how the scriptures were written; mankind is 5,000 to 6,000 years in history. How long did Adam and Eve live before they sinned? How many years did they walk with God in complete perfection before they finally disobeyed? No one knows. It could have been a matter of weeks or it could have been many years, but regardless of that, they failed, they sinned, they took of the forbidden fruit that God commanded them not to take.

You and I plus eight billion additional people on the planet, and all the billions that lived before us have all paid the price of the sin and disobedience of Adam and Eve. Every day we go to work, and we work by the sweat of our brow. Women have the curse of pain in childbearing and many of those women work an outside job as well.

Why did Adam and Eve do this? The answer is simple. Was it their appetite? They felt the need or desire to experience something that was forbidden. Appetite is not always about eating. We overeat because we are not in control of our eating appetite, and people commit adultery because they are not in control of their sexual appetite. People covet and steal because they are not in control of their appetite to possess things. With all the surrounding beauty, the trees, the flowers, waterfalls, rivers, streams, oceans, and all the food they could want or need, was there at their fingertips. On that tragic and dreary day, Eve walked over to the tree where she was forbidden to eat, and the serpent speaks to her about the forbidden fruit. He lied to her, and she believed every word. Did she believe the serpent because Adam failed to explain the commandment of God, or was she willfully disobedient? We do not know for sure. One thing we do know, their appetite was out of control.

Gen 2:16-18 And the Lord God commanded the man, saying, Of every tree of the garden thou mayest freely eat:
17 But of the tree of the knowledge of good and evil, thou shalt not eat of it: for in the day that thou eatest thereof thou shalt surely die.
18 And the Lord God said, It is not good that the man should be alone; I will make him an help meet for him.

Gen 2:21-22 And the Lord God caused a deep sleep to fall upon Adam, and he slept: and he took one

of his ribs, and closed up the flesh instead thereof;

22 And the rib, which the Lord God had taken from man, made he a woman, and brought her unto the man.

Gen 3:1-7 Now the serpent was more subtil than any beast of the field which the Lord God had made. And he said unto the woman, Yea, hath God said, Ye shall not eat of every tree of the garden?

2 And the woman said unto the serpent, We may eat of the fruit of the trees of the garden:

3 But of the fruit of the tree which is in the midst of the garden, God hath said, Ye shall not eat of it, neither shall ye touch it, lest ye die.

4 And the serpent said unto the woman, Ye shall not surely die:

5 For God doth know that in the day ye eat thereof, then your eyes shall be opened, and ye shall be as gods, knowing good and evil.

6 And when the woman saw that the tree was good for food, and that it was pleasant to the eyes, and a tree

to be desired to make one wise, she took of the fruit thereof, and did eat, and gave also unto her husband with her; and he did eat.

7 And the eyes of them both were opened, and they knew that they were naked; and they sewed fig leaves together, and made themselves aprons.

Gen 3:16-19 Unto the woman he said, I will greatly multiply thy sorrow and thy conception; in sorrow thou shalt bring forth children; and thy desire shall be to thy husband, and he shall rule over thee.

17 And unto Adam he said, Because thou hast hearkened unto the voice of thy wife, and hast eaten of the tree, of which I commanded thee, saying, Thou shalt not eat of it: cursed is the ground for thy sake; in sorrow shalt thou eat of it all the days of thy life;

18 Thorns also and thistles shall it bring forth to thee; and thou shalt eat the herb of the field;

19 In the sweat of thy face shalt thou eat bread, till thou return unto the ground; for out of it wast thou taken: for dust thou art, and unto dust shalt thou return.

Another great human failure is the story of Esau. Twins by the names of Esau and Jacob were by nature at odds with one another. Esau was a man of the field where Jacob was more of a businessman. Esau's birthright was a great blessing. The firstborn son of every family was to receive the birthright. You will be blessed to know the details of a birthright. I would recommend doing a study on that.

There was a day that Esau was out hunting, and he came home after many hours without a kill. He was hungry and famished. His brother Jacob being quite the trickster was ready to get something for free if possible. Esau could smell the pottage that Jacob had on the fire and was quite impressed. Jacob asked for a bowl of the soup, but Jacob declined to give him any. Esau did not value his birthright. He lived for instant gratification. Jacob may or may not have known that Esau did not value his birthright, but he threw out a temptation and said, "Trade me your birthright for this bowl of soup". With some discussion, Esau finally gave in. He was willing to trade his valuable birthright for a bowl of pottage.

Your Salvation is your birthright. What is the value you place on it? How do you protect it?

What gratification, sin or thrill would you trade your birthright for? Some have sold their birthright for a one-night stand and others have traded it daily for those little white lies they tell. It is all about the appetite that we have, or we are not supposed to have; the forbidden fruit.

If you were to ask the average Christian who his greatest enemy was, they would probably say "the devil". Well, the devil truly is a great foe, but he is not our biggest enemy. You are your greatest enemy. Your flesh gives you more trouble than anyone. Most of your temptations come from the lust of your flesh. If there was no devil, you would probably not even notice it. Our sinful nature is powerful. It wants its way. It is selfish, jealous, bitter, angry, lustful, prideful, and has a host of other carnal ways and thoughts.

Gal 5:16-17 This I say then, Walk in the Spirit, and ye shall not fulfil the lust of the flesh.
17 For the flesh lusteth against the Spirit, and the Spirit against the flesh: and these are contrary the one to the other: so that ye cannot do the things that ye would.

Gal 5:19-21 Now the works of the flesh are manifest, which are these; Adultery, fornication, uncleanness, lasciviousness,
20 Idolatry, witchcraft, hatred, variance, emulations, wrath, strife, seditions, heresies,
21 Envyings, murders, drunkenness, revellings, and such like: of the which I tell you before, as I have also told you in time past, that they which do such things shall not inherit the kingdom of God.

These "works of the flesh" are trouble within themselves. When the enemy pounces on one of those fleshly natures within you and, begins to irritate it and tempt it even more, then you have more problems. But This is why the Bible teaches fasting. Fasting is the key to keeping under our body and bringing it into subjection.

1 Cor 9:27 But I keep under my body, and bring it into subjection: lest that by any means, when I have preached to others, I myself should be a castaway.

The Apostle Paul mentioned warfare. He said there is a warfare in my members. It is the fight of flesh against the Spirit and the Spirit against the flesh. The flesh has hostility toward God. The flesh is the enemy of God. The Apostle also taught to be temperate in all things. Without a disciplined life, we do not differ from the world. The flesh must die to the will of the Spirit. We live in a socializing, eating, drinking, making merry world.

Rom 7:23-24 But I see another law in my members, warring against the law of my mind, and bringing me into captivity to the law of sin which is in my members.

24 O wretched man that I am. who shall deliver me from the body of this death?

Look at this phrase by the Apostle, "who shall deliver me from the body of this death". History says that the ruthless Romans would take a person who committed a terrible crime and take a dead body and tie the dead body to the living person, face to face. And for a time, he would suffer face to face having this dead body rotting on his human flesh. History says that this is the reference Paul was thinking about. "Who shall deliver me from the body of this death" or I could say it in our vernacular. "who shall deliver me from this dead body". Yes, if you got the picture here, living for God in the Spirit is like having a dead body connected to us. We can be as Spiritual as possible but that flesh, that carnality is still there. It can be under subjection, but any length of time without prayer and fasting could suddenly allow that old man to rise in carnality.

1 Cor 9:24-27 Know ye not that they which run in a race run all, but one receiveth the prize? So run, that ye may obtain.

25 And every man that striveth for the mastery is temperate in all things. Now they do it to obtain a corruptible crown; but we an incorruptible.

26 I therefore so run, not as uncertainly; so fight I, not as one that beateth the air:

27 But I keep under my body, and bring it into subjection: lest that by any means, when I have preached to others, I myself should be a castaway.

I want to show you several Bible versions of 1 Corinthians 9:27. They are quite enlightening.

1 Cor 9:27 but I discipline my body and make it my slave, so that, after I have preached to others, I myself will not be disqualified. NASU

1 Cor 9:27 but I buffet my body, and bring it into bondage: lest by any means, after that I have preached to others, I myself should be rejected. ASV

1 Cor 9:27 But I give blows to my body, and keep it under control, for fear that, after having given the good news to others, I myself might not have God's approval. BBE

1 Cor 9:27 but I hit hard and straight at my own body and lead it off into slavery, lest possibly, after I have been a herald to others, I should myself be rejected. Weymouth

Look at the comments in Vincent's Word Studies on verse 27. "I keep under" hupoopiazoo. A feeble translation, and missing the metaphor. The word means "to strike under the eye; to give one a black eye." It occurs elsewhere in the New Testament but once, Luke 18:5 (see note). The English Revised Version (1885): "I buffet." The blow of the trained boxer was the more formidable from the use of the "cestus," consisting of ox-hide bands covered with knots and nails, and loaded with lead and iron. So Entellus throws Iris boxing-gloves into the ring, formed of seven bulls'-hides with lead and iron sewed into them (Virgil, "Aeneid," v., 405). They were sometimes called guiotoroi, "limb-breakers." A most interesting account is given by Rodolfo Lanziani, "Ancient Rome in the Light of Recent Discoveries," of the exhuming at the foundation of the Temple of the Sun, erected by Aurelian, of a sitting bronze statue of a boxer. The accompanying photograph shows the construction of the fur-lined boxing gloves secured by thongs wound around the forearm half-way to the elbow. The gloves cover the thumb and the hand to the first finger-joints. The writer says; "The nose is swollen from the effects of the last blow received; the ears resemble a fiat and shapeless piece of leather; the neck, the shoulders, the breast, are seamed with scars... The details of the fur-lined boxing-gloves are also interesting, and one wonders how any human being, no matter how strong and powerful, could stand the blows from such weapons as these gloves, made of four or five thicknesses of leather, and fortified with brass knuckles." "Bring it into subjection" doulagoogoo. The English Revised Version (1885): "bring it into bondage." Metaphor of captives after battle. Not of leading the vanquished round the arena (so Godet), a custom of which there is no trace, and which, in most cases, the condition of the vanquished would render impossible. It is rather one of those sudden changes and mixtures of metaphor so frequent in Paul's writings. See, for instance, 2 Cor 5:1-2. (from Vincent's Word Studies in the New Testament, Electronic Database. Copyright © 1997, 2003, 2005, 2006 by Biblesoft, Inc. All rights reserved.)

So yes, we are talking about fasting and prayer. Let me point out two things that stand out in Vincents Word Studies. "to strike under the eye". When you are fasting, you are in a sense, striking yourself under the eye. You are beating yourself repeatedly with the fist.

"bring it into bondage", "captives after battle". After fasting, when your flesh is under subjection, it is your captive, it is in bondage to you "after the battle". The history here of boxing, the gloves, and being buffeted is amazing. It shows how Paul felt about keeping his body in subjection to God. Let me point out also the word "buffeted". We might think of waxing a car, but it means "to beat repeatedly with the fist". As the Greek says, "to strike under the eye".

Some people do not want to fast because it makes them feel bad. They get a headache or whatever, so they do not fast. You are not supposed to feel good when you fast. Though after some time, usually about three days of a water fast, you will feel better and strength will come to you. Fasting pushes the flesh down and keeps it down so it is not reigning as king on the throne of your life. You can feed the flesh, or you can feed the Spirit. The one you feed the most is the one that will win. You have heard of the two dogs. One dog was black, and the other white. They were fighting, and no one seemed to win in this fight until one of the dogs was fed by its master. So, it is with you and me. The white dog represents good and the black dog represents evil and, the one you feed the most is the one that will win.

Rom 8:5-9 For they that are after the flesh do mind the things of the flesh; but they that are after the Spirit the things of the Spirit.
6 For to be carnally minded is death; but to be spiritually minded is life and peace.
7 Because the carnal mind is enmity against God: for it is not subject to

the law of God, neither indeed can be.
8 So then they that are in the flesh cannot please God.
9 But ye are not in the flesh, but in the Spirit, if so be that the Spirit of God dwell in you. Now if any man have not the Spirit of Christ, he is none of his.

Rom 8:12-13 Therefore, brethren, we are debtors, not to the flesh, to live after the flesh.
13 For if ye live after the flesh, ye shall die: but if ye through the Spirit do mortify the deeds of the body, ye shall live.

When you abstain from the earthly, it opens the door to a new realm. When you stop feeding the flesh everything it wants, then the heavenly realm can open up to you and, you can walk into it. At that point, miracles, signs, wonders, dreams, and visions from God can open up to you. What do you hunger for the most? God still rewards sacrifice. As the Bible says, obedience is better than sacrifice, but the neat thing here is that fasting needs to be obeyed and followed in a biblical pattern. When the example of fasting from the Bible is obeyed, the heavenly realm will open in new dimensions. Is there a direct command in the Bible to fast? I do not believe so, but there are enough strong hints and recommendations to fast that there is no excuse to live in the flesh. Fasting is a lost art. It is a lost sacrifice and discipline. It is self-denial in the greatest form.

Luke 14:26-27 If any man come to me, and hate not his father, and mother, and wife, and children, and brethren, and sisters, yea, and his own life also, he cannot be my disciple.
27 And whosoever doth not bear his cross, and come after me, cannot be my disciple.

If we are not careful, we want to love everybody and everything equal to God. Jesus said to take up your cross and to deny yourself and even your family. It does not mean that you do not love them, but it means to love them less than God. Self-denial is part of walking with the Lord. Fasting takes the scepter from the flesh and puts it in the hand of God. Servanthood and submission begin with repentance. We must become servants before we can become heirs, children, kings, and priests. Jesus loves sinners, so much as to eat with them. We love ourselves too much. We ignore the Sinner. Why do some congregations stare at the sinner when they walk in? Too many Christians involved are involved only in the flesh. There is no power, no virtue. They have only a verbal witness, if that. We should move in the power of Acts chapter one verse eight but, we cannot if there is no deep consecration through fasting and prayer.

Acts 1:8 But ye shall receive power, after that the Holy Ghost is come upon you: and ye shall be witnesses unto me both in Jerusalem, and in all Judæa, and in Samaria, and unto the uttermost part of the earth.

John 3:30-31 He must increase, but I must decrease.
31 He that cometh from above is above all: he that is of the earth is earthly, and speaketh of the earth: he that cometh from heaven is above all.

We know what John the Baptist was saying here, "I must decrease in popularity", "the attention must go from myself to the Christ". You must decrease. You must decrease in fleshly desires and fleshly control. He must be the Lord on your throne. He must reign as King in your life.

You can decrease in the flesh and when you do, you will increase in the Spirit, or rather, Jesus will increase in you and through you. In the flesh, we disconnect from God, but through fasting and prayer, we reconnect with God. When disconnected from God, our faith diminishes, and miracles are few.

We live in a world of pleasure and entertainment. The flesh wants to be appeased and satisfied. The carnal mind wants entertainment, entertainment that takes away from your faith. Worldly entertainment increases self and decreases Christ in you. Therefore, it is so vital to have times of consecration with days of fasting. Fasting not just food, but all worldly entertainment. I understand that not all entertainment is sinful, but during the fast, all carnal desires must die. We must die to self. This is the only way we can please God and have faith pleasing to God.

Heb 11:6 But without faith it is impossible to please him: for he that cometh to God must believe that he, is and that he is a rewarder of them that diligently seek him.

Rom 8:6-8 For to be carnally minded is death; but to be spiritually minded is life and peace.
7 Because the carnal mind is enmity against God: for it is not subject to the law of God, neither indeed can be.
8 So then they that are in the flesh cannot please God.

Wow, what a powerful passage here in Romans. The carnal/fleshly mind breeds death. The spiritual mind is life. The carnal mind is the enemy of God and will not submit to the ways of God. Because of this, we fast and pray that we may be transformed and renewed in our minds/thoughts.

Rom 12:2 And be not conformed to this world: but be ye transformed by

**the renewing of your mind, that ye
may prove what is that good, and
acceptable, and perfect, will of God.**

You will never earn or deserve a miracle or
God's grace. Fasting is for oneself to humble
his flesh and come under subjection to the
Spirit. Fasting will not twist God's arm. It will
not persuade God. Your rising faith through
fasting will move the hand of Almighty God
on your behalf. If we are not fasting, no
doubt carnality is running rampant. Eve was
tempted through her stomach. Her lust for
food caused her to sin. Some are hooked on
drugs and some addicted to food. They
cannot control their appetite. The apostle
Paul knew some like that. He referenced
them like the following.

**Titus 1:12 One of themselves, even a
prophet of their own, said, The
Cretians are alway liars, evil beasts,
slow bellies.**

The term "slow bellies" means "lazy
gluttons". These people cannot control their
appetites. Their appetite controls them.
The flesh wants to be gratified and fulfilled.
When you are given to prayer and fasting,

few things move you. You care little for how you can be fulfilled. You want revival and you want to walk under an open Heaven.

1 Cor 6:12 All things are lawful unto me, but all things are not expedient: all things are lawful for me, but I will not be brought under the power of any. KJV

1 Cor 6:12 "All things are lawful for me," but not all things are helpful. "All things are lawful for me," but I will not be dominated by anything. ESV

A powerful verse there. Look also at the ESV , "I will not be dominated by anything". The Christian should be without any addiction. Remember, the addiction to food will keep you from fasting. This addiction can open other addictions. Regardless of what has a hold on you today, it can be broken. It can be a long-standing addiction in your life. It may be an emotional weight you carry. With correct fasting, all things are possible to him that believes.

Jer 5:7-8 How shall I pardon thee for this? thy children have forsaken me, and sworn by them that are no gods: when I had fed them to the full, they then committed adultery, and assembled themselves by troops in the harlots' houses.
8 They were as fed horses in the morning: every one neighed after his neighbour's wife.

Look at this. God says, "I had fed them to the full". This is referring to feeding them all the food they wanted. Look at the results of it:

1. Thy children have forsaken me
2. Their children are worshipping false gods
3. They committed adultery
4. They assembled with prostitutes
5. Every one neighed after his neighbor's wife

Is this what we want? We do not want to be controlled by the flesh and the lusts thereof. Fasting will defeat these kinds of desires. Your flesh will become obedient to the Spirit. Studies have been done that show the direct connection of the arousal of the taste buds to the arousal of sexual desires. The lack of control in one's eating habits can get him in trouble especially that of the lust of the flesh.

Gal 5:16-21 This I say then, Walk in the Spirit, and ye shall not fulfil the lust of the flesh.
17 For the flesh lusteth against the Spirit, and the Spirit against the flesh: and these are contrary the one to the other: so that ye cannot do the things that ye would.
18 But if ye be led of the Spirit, ye are not under the law.
19 Now the works of the flesh are manifest, which are these; Adultery, fornication, uncleanness, lasciviousness,
20 Idolatry, witchcraft, hatred, variance, emulations, wrath, strife, seditions, heresies,
21 Envyings, murders, drunkenness, revellings, and such like: of the which I tell you before, as I have also told you in time past, that they which do such things shall not inherit the kingdom of God.

Any sin is possible when walking in the flesh and any miracle is possible when walking in the Spirit. You will have trouble walking in the Spirit, (if not impossible) without the spiritual discipline of fasting.

You will have faith in the Spirit (God) when the flesh is dead. The voice of God will become louder than the voice of the flesh. Carnality is the wall between us and God that keeps us from hearing from God. Fasting with prayer tears down that wall and the voice of Jesus becomes clear. Praise and worship, as important as it is, will not do much to this wall of flesh. Bible reading and study will do some damage to the wall of flesh. Sacrificial prayer can knock some enormous holes in that wall, but fasting can, with these others combined, tear down that wall completely. In the Spirit you are unstoppable. Your faith will rise to a new high. You will bypass all high watermarks in the Spirit with a regular regiment of fasting in your life. This I call fasting faith.

We will not get our miracle, our revival in the fleshly realm. It will have to happen in the Spirit. A church can get a large crowd attending, but was it a revival of the Spirit or a "revival of the flesh"? The flesh is easily attracted to the bright, colorful, flashing lights, the smoke machines, but in the Spirit, we will see the lame walk, blind to see and deaf to hear. This was the revival in the New Testament.

As, long as the flesh rules and reigns, faith cannot emerge, grow, and react with much velocity. The limited faith in the northern hemisphere does not seem so bad or so weak until we see the results of faith in more poor countries. We are inundated with fake faith, false prophets vying for the people's money. "Send me $44.44 for a bottle of anointed water from the Jordan river". With that, we are so pressured to "keep up with the Jones'", the newest cars, the biggest house, and the largest salary we can get. Is there anything wrong with these things? No, but these can things hinder our faith. Do you publish your fast days? Do you let the world know you push back the plate? If so, the flesh may want glory for even the fast you are doing.

Matt 6:6 But thou, when thou prayest, enter into thy closet, and when thou hast shut thy door, pray

to thy Father which is in secret; and thy Father which seeth in secret shall reward thee openly.

Rom 16:18 For they that are such serve not our Lord Jesus Christ, but their own belly; and by good words and fair speeches deceive the hearts of the simple.

The apostle again points out that some serve "their belly". The lust for food is a great deceiver. The lust for food is associated also with the lust for power, fame, control, uncontrolled sexual desires, and more. A three day water fast can kill out a lot of this. Once the flesh is controlled though fasting, we need a regular regiment of fasting to maintain victory over carnality.

Ezek 16:49-50 Behold, this was the iniquity of thy sister Sodom, pride, fulness of bread, and abundance of idleness was in her and in her daughters, neither did she strengthen the hand of the poor and needy.
50 And they were haughty, and committed abomination before me:

therefore I took them away as I saw good.

What were the iniquities of Sodom?

- Pride

- Fulness of bread

- Abundance of idleness

Imagine this, God makes fulness of bread equal to pride. Do not make this some typology. It is not. The #2 sin of Sodom was overeating. The sin of sodomy is not even mentioned here. Why? Because there were sins, that led to sodomy. No one wakes up in the morning after living a very moral lifestyle and, decides to commit sodomy. One thing leads to another. Sin leads to more sin. Sin leads to deeper sin. We would not call fulness of bread iniquity, but God did. What we call small sins leads to depravity and wickedness. When the stomach calls the shots, anything is possible. Bad eating habits is iniquity. Overeating as a lifestyle is iniquity. They add sin to sin.

Isa 30:1 Woe to the rebellious children, saith the Lord, that take

counsel, but not of me; and that cover with a covering, but not of my spirit, that they may add sin to sin:

Prov 30:9 Lest I be full, and deny thee, and say, Who is the Lord? or lest I be poor, and steal, and take the name of my God in vain.

"Lest I be full, and deny thee", wow. The impact of overeating has on our spirit man is amazing. Will we be denying the Lord because we get full at dinner? No. This is talking about someone who is out of control. He does not eat to live but lives to eat. There is nothing wrong with eating good and enjoying a tasty meal but eating like you are going to the electric chair every meal may be a problem. Is overeating a spiritual problem? No. the spiritual problem is causing the gluttony. He has become a victim of the lust for food.

Rom 8:12-13 Therefore, brethren, we are debtors, not to the flesh, to live after the flesh.
13 For if ye live after the flesh, ye shall die: but if ye through the Spirit

**do mortify the deeds of the body, ye
shall live.**

**Matt 16:24 Then said Jesus unto his
disciples, If any man will come after
me, let him deny himself, and take
up his cross, and follow me.**

This human nature must be put down. We
cannot expect to see exploits or even go to
Heaven if we walk in the flesh and never
deny ourselves of what the "old man" wants.
You have two natures. You know, that is, if
you have the Holy Spirit. The divine nature
can only have control if the carnal nature
dies. Your human nature is there, and it is
your responsibility to keep it under control
so the Holy Spirit can rule and reign in your
daily life.

**2 Peter 1:4 Whereby are given unto
us exceeding great and precious
promises: that by these ye might be
partakers of the divine nature,
having escaped the corruption that
is in the world through lust.**

4 / SECRETS OF DANIEL'S 21 DAY BATTLE IN THE HEAVINLIES

In this study, we will learn of the invisible battle behind the scenes when you fast. There may be a literal hand to hand battle in the angelic realm. You may not see it or even know about it, but when you set your heart to seek the Lord by prayer and fasting, something is happening. Maybe an angel has been sent to assist you. Maybe God has put you on someone's heart to pray just for you. The miracle you are to receive could very well depend on your fast. You must know this. You must understand the seriousness of the invisible. We live in a visible, fleshly, tangible realm but, in the spirit, we must see further. We must know more. By faith, we understand that something is changing, breaking, or being revealed. You cannot truly seek God without something taking place. Do not fret when you cannot see it. We see God do miracles days or weeks after a fast and, no doubt the fast had something to do with it, but we disconnect that thought because it was not immediate.

Dan 10:2-3 In those days I Daniel was mourning three full weeks.

3 I ate no pleasant bread, neither came flesh nor wine in my mouth, neither did I anoint myself at all, till three whole weeks were fulfilled.

Dan 10:5-8 Then I lifted up mine eyes, and looked, and behold a certain man clothed in linen, whose loins were girded with fine gold of Uphaz:

6 His body also was like the beryl, and his face as the appearance of lightning, and his eyes as lamps of fire, and his arms and his feet like in colour to polished brass, and the voice of his words like the voice of a multitude.

7 And I Daniel alone saw the vision: for the men that were with me saw not the vision; but a great quaking fell upon them, so that they fled to hide themselves. 8 Therefore I was left alone, and saw this great vision, and there remained no strength in me: for my comeliness was turned in me into corruption, and I retained no strength.

When I read verses 5 and 6, I want to think this was the Lord himself coming to Daniel, but later verses make me think it was an angel that came to him. These two verses give an amazing description of this visitor. So, in the fast, this heavenly visitor comes to Daniel in a vision. This was such a powerful scene that the men with him experienced a "great quaking". Was it their own personal earthquake, or was it something in their emotions they experienced? Someone might say that the angel in verse five is God because of the amazing description of him. It seems that way, but I have to doubt that, since he needed help. The angel Michael came to help him in verse 13.

Dan 10:9-12 Yet heard I the voice of his words: and when I heard the voice of his words, then was I in a deep sleep on my face, and my face toward the ground. 10 And, behold, an hand touched me, which set me upon my knees and upon the palms of my hands.
11 And he said unto me, O Daniel, a man greatly beloved, understand the words that I speak unto thee,

**and stand upright: for unto thee am
I now sent. And when he had spoken
this word unto me, I stood
trembling.
12 Then said he unto me, Fear not,
Daniel: for from the first day that
thou didst set thine heart to
understand, and to chasten thyself
before thy God, thy words were
heard, and I am come for thy words.**

Daniel was put into some trance or had
passed out. He was in a "deep sleep". The
heavenly visitor awoke him and raised him
to his knees and said to him "Stand up". And
while Daniel stood trembling, the angel said,
"from the first day...thy words were heard".
And yes, you, when you chasten yourself
before God, He sees and hears. You may not
be thinking so but, we need to trust and
know this truth. The man Daniel was no
better or special than us, but he made
himself noticeable by prayer and fasting.
God took notice and sent a messenger.

**Dan 10:13-17 But the prince of the
kingdom of Persia withstood me one
and twenty days: but, lo, Michael,
one of the chief princes, came to**

help me; and I remained there with the kings of Persia.

14 Now I am come to make thee understand what shall befall thy people in the latter days: for yet the vision is for many days.

15 And when he had spoken such words unto me, I set my face toward the ground, and I became dumb.

16 And, behold, one like the similitude of the sons of men touched my lips: then I opened my mouth, and spake, and said unto him that stood before me, O my lord, by the vision my sorrows are turned upon me, and I have retained no strength.

17 For how can the servant of this my lord talk with this my lord? for as for me, straightway there remained no strength in me, neither is there breath left in me.

Who is the prince of Persia? Was he a man? No. this is referring to a spiritual prince. A demon spirit that was ruling the kingdom of Persia in that era. The angel that came to Daniel says that the prince of Persia withstood him 21 days (v. 13) but, another angel comes by the name of Michael to fight against the prince of Persia. So now it is two against one. They now outnumber the evil spirit over Persia. Until Michael came, it seemed to be in a stalemate. What gave the breakthrough for this second angel by the name of Michael to get there? The answer is, the fasting of Daniel. He did not give up or give in. Daniel knew nothing of this unseen battle until the first angel revealed himself to tell the story.

Now that there is a breakthrough, Daniel gets the message from the first angel. That message would have never gotten through without the second angel's (Michael) help and the continued fast that opened that unseen doorway. Fasting opens the door to the heavenly realm for needed deliverance. You may never know or have the outcome of a situation revealed to you, but you must trust God. He could use you around the world as a spiritual missionary. This is so important in the ministry of fasting and intercessory prayer. You may be a, secret weapon in the hands of our General.

Let us tie in verse 16. This is the third angel in the passage. "one like the similitude of the sons of men..."

In my first experience with angels, one night, sound asleep, I was awakened and immediately went into intercessory prayer. I was very awake, which never happens in the middle of the night for me. I got out of bed and walked, praying with a substantial burden, and strongly speaking in tongues. After a little time of this, I became very weak and went down on my knees, still speaking in tongues. Suddenly, I felt a firm hand on my shoulder. I did not see him, but I know that was an angel that came to me that night. For what reason, I do not know. All I can say is, he possibly came to strengthen me, for I was in a spiritual battle that had been ongoing for some time.

Luke 22:43-44 And there appeared an angel unto him from heaven, strengthening him.
44 And being in an agony he prayed more earnestly: and his sweat was as it were great drops of blood falling down to the ground.

Here it is where Jesus is in the garden before His betrayal, praying. An angel came and ministered to Him to strengthen Him and He could pray more earnestly.

Dan 10:18-20 Then there came again and touched me one like the appearance of a man, and he strengthened me,
19 And said, O man greatly beloved, fear not: peace be unto thee, be strong, yea, be strong. And when he had spoken unto me, I was strengthened, and said, Let my lord speak; for thou hast strengthened me.
20 Then said he, Knowest thou wherefore I come unto thee? and now will I return to fight with the prince of Persia: and when I am gone forth, lo, the prince of Grecia shall come.

We can see here in verse 18 how the angel gave Daniel strength. He tells Daniel in verse 20 that he is leaving to fight again with the demon prince of Persia and when he leaves, the prince demon of Grecia will come. Another point to make is, the angel in verse

18 is the same as the one in verse 16. "Then there came again". God sent the answer to Daniel, but the answer through the angel did not and could not get through until he pushed back the plate. A lower faith level hinders the answer but, fasting raises the faith level and the answer can get through.

The invisible war is veritable. It is more real than what is happening in the natural human realm. One realm, the spiritual or human realm, can affect the other. A person of fasting affects the spirit realm by causing breakthroughs and deliverances. A person of carnality with actions of sin can cause more demonic activity in his life and the lives of others.

Job 23:12 Neither have I gone back from the commandment of his lips; I have esteemed the words of his mouth more than my necessary food.

This powerful Bible verse here in the book of Job adds to the teaching we find in the book of Daniel about his fast, the "Daniel's fast". We could say here that Job understood the difference between gorging himself and eating only what was necessary, "My necessary food". I want to make another point about this spiritual battle between the three angels and the two fallen demonic spirits. Look at the next verse in Psalms. The word "delivereth" has a firm agreement with the story here in Daniel.

Ps 34:7 The angel of the Lord encampeth round about them that fear him, and delivereth them.

OT:2502 to equip (for war), to arm for war, to rescue (from The Online Bible Thayer's Greek Lexicon and Brown Driver & Briggs Hebrew Lexicon, Copyright © 1993.

Look at this, "to equip (for war), to arm for war"... Your angel is armed as Daniel's angel, to fight in war. He is equipped for battle. Let us look at the fast itself.

Dan 10:2-3 In those days I Daniel was mourning three full weeks.
3 I ate no pleasant bread, neither came flesh nor wine in my mouth, neither did I anoint myself at all, till three whole weeks were fulfilled.

It truly looks as if Daniel ate during the twenty-one days but, limited eating to things that did not appeal to the taste buds. "I ate no pleasant bread, neither came flesh nor wine in my mouth". Daniel may have had the custom to deny himself of certain foods. We see earlier in the book how he and the three Hebrew children resisted the king of the lavish food he wanted to feed them. I am not insinuating that Daniel was a vegetarian, but no doubt was used to this discipline.

Dan 1:8 But Daniel purposed in his heart that he would not defile himself with the portion of the king's meat, nor with the wine which he drank: therefore he requested of the prince of the eunuchs that he might not defile himself.

Dan 1:11-12 Then said Daniel to Melzar, whom the prince of the eunuchs had set over Daniel, Hananiah, Mishael, and Azariah,
12 Prove thy servants, I beseech thee, ten days; and let them give us pulse to eat, and water to drink.

We see here that Daniel asked for a replacement of the king's dish for pulse (vegetables) and water for the ten days. The wise man in the next verse writes about eating control. The word "drunkenness" is about overeating. You can get full of vegetables but the fulness does not last long. Maybe Daniel was eating for strength for the twenty-one days so he could do his work and seek the Lord as he needed too. Why was he fasting? He had previously seen a vision but, did not understand it. He had set his heart on getting the interpretation.

Eccl 10:17 Blessed art thou, O land, when thy king is the son of nobles, and thy princes eat in due season, for strength, and not for drunkenness.

The custom with most of us is to determine a certain number of days to fast. It is commonly believed that Daniel scheduled a twenty-one-day fast. I do not believe he did. I believe he fasted until the answer came. Let me show you why.

Dan 10:2-3 In those days I Daniel was mourning three full weeks.

3 I ate no pleasant bread, neither came flesh nor wine in my mouth, neither did I anoint myself at all, till three whole weeks were fulfilled.

Verse two and three do not say he pre-planned the fast of twenty-one days. He just tells what happened, after the fact.

Dan 10:13 But the prince of the kingdom of Persia withstood me one and twenty days: but, lo, Michael, one of the chief princes, came to help me; and I remained there with the kings of Persia.

Here the angel tells him what happened in the spirit realm. He was "withstood twenty-one days". The angels defeated the demon after that many days. It was a fight in the spirit realm. The breakthrough by the angels, just happened to take place after three weeks. The fast could not have been planned. Daniel did not know how long it would take to get the victory. It all depended on the battle in the unseen world. The battle lasted three weeks with victory for Daniel. If Daniel had not fasted, he either would not have gotten the victory, or it would have taken much longer. Daniel was "fasting through", just like we talk about "praying through".

5 / SECRETS OF FAITH, POWER, & BOLDNESS

What we need is, is an extreme faith for extreme problems. Let me say here that faith in God, the power of God, and boldness all work together. It is our faith that will show the power of God and it is boldness on our part that will cause our faith to act. Without action, there will be no miracle because faith without works is dead.

James 2:20 But wilt thou know, O vain man, that faith without works is dead?

James 2:18 Yea, a man may say, Thou hast faith, and I have works: shew me thy faith without thy works, and I will shew thee my faith by my works.

It is easy to say "I believe" but is there action to prove it? Another point here is, does God make a promise and then not do it? Should we call God a liar or would it be more honest to say, "my faith in this situation is deficient"? Now, I will admit that I do not understand everything and do not understand how God operates in all He does, but He honors faith and is moved by faith. They carried the man with the palsy to the roof of a house. The roof was broke-open by his four friends and then he was let down to where Jesus was. Now, that is faith in action.

Heb 6:18 That by two immutable things, in which it was impossible for God to lie, we might have a strong consolation, who have fled for refuge to lay hold upon the hope set before us:

God cannot lie. It is impossible. So then, we need boldness to act. In Acts chapter three, Peter and John showed action with their bold faith. Yes, with boldness they took the lame man by the hand... the result was a miracle.

Acts 4:29-31 And now, Lord, behold their threatenings: and grant unto thy servants, that with all boldness they may speak thy word,
30 By stretching forth thine hand to heal; and that signs and wonders

may be done by the name of thy holy child Jesus.
31 And when they had prayed, the place was shaken where they were assembled together; and they were all filled with the Holy Ghost, and they spake the word of God with boldness.

We pray for revival, but the early church prayed for boldness. In verse 29 they prayed for boldness, and in verse 31 they spoke with boldness. Without faith, there will be power and no act of boldness. In Acts, Paul was teaching and perceived that a certain lame man had faith. He, in boldness, told him to stand up. The lame man stood up. The power of God flowed through his faith and his act of faith.

Some years ago, on my way to and from work, I would pass a certain tavern or club (maybe a strip club) on the south side of Chicago. One day as I drove by it, I pointed at it and said, "in the name of Jesus Christ, burn down and do not be rebuilt." I did this off and on for several months. One day passing by, I looked that way and saw a heap of charred rubble. It had burned to the ground.

It amazed me! It happened. Sometime later they built there on that spot. I can joyfully say that a Burger King stands there today. God performed the miracle as I spoke it. I had another situation similar to that. In the 1990s, I was working on a new church plant near to that location there in Chicago. Every week my mother and I would gather to pray for the city of Calumet City, IL. We agreed in prayer and the command of faith, that God would "dry up" the city. It was known for many taverns and strip joints. At one point it had over 300 in a city of 30,000 people. So, each week we bound the spirits that had taken this city so many decades earlier. We would command the alcohol spirits to leave and clubs to shut down in Jesus' name. This went on for some months and then one day the newspaper came out with big bold headlines "Mayor so and so is buying up the taverns in the city and will bulldoze them to the ground." Our prayers were working. Some months later, the trucks and bulldozers began knocking down one tavern after another. Over the next couple of years, many taverns came down and every strip club as far as I know also came down. There was one area of several blocks where it was one bar after another. Today that area is flat except for a few newer businesses. There are very few taverns in that city. Yes, with fasting, prayer, and boldness, God can work through you in your city. He is looking for partners.

We have all the power we need or ever will need, but many times we do not have the faith to get the job done. It is like a fast race car. It has a powerful motor but if it does not have the fuel; the power is useless. Faith is like that fuel. If our gas tank is empty, the motor will not start.

John 14:12-14 Verily, verily, I say unto you, He that believeth on me, the works that I do shall he do also; and greater works than these shall he do; because I go unto my Father.
13 And whatsoever ye shall ask in my name, that will I do, that the Father may be glorified in the Son.
14 If ye shall ask any thing in my name, I will do it.

Jesus said "greater works" not fewer works. You are reading this book because of your hunger for "greater works". I do not think you are interested in how to get hungry, but if it takes that, you are willing. You believe the Bible and will do whatever it takes to rise above this world and its unbelief.

The wonder of consistent fasting with prayer is at, all times you can expect the miraculous to happen. Consistency in these holy deeds can open the heavens, that wherever you go, you can be a vessel and a tool in the hand of the almighty. Why go on a fast and then end it with carnality and lose everything you have gained? Why get to a place of sensitivity with God and then crash into a wall of flesh and carnality? Keep your gains. Keep it with consistent prayer. Not that you need to go on a seven-day fast every week or two, but you can have a maintenance of fasting to keep yourself under subjection. You know the intercessor is not the funniest guy in the room. He is not the person vying for everyone's attention. There is a faith he must maintain. A submission he must hold on to.

Consistency is important in these holy deeds. Look at Cornelius in Acts. His consistency brought a message from an angel. Everyone in his house got saved because of his seeking God. Even the atheist cries out to God in times of great distress. He blames the God he does not believe in when tragedy hits his home.

Acts 10:1-4 There was a certain man in Cæsarea called Cornelius, a centurion of the band called the Italian band,
2 A devout man, and one that feared God with all his house, which gave much alms to the people, and prayed to God alway.
3 He saw in a vision evidently about the ninth hour of the day an angel of God coming into him, and saying unto him, Cornelius.
4 And when he looked on him, he was afraid, and said, What is it, Lord? And he said unto him, Thy prayers and thine alms are come up for a memorial before God.

The sacrifice of fasting is more than just a way to humble oneself, it is and should be an inroad into the supernatural. So many times, not that the miracle is being held back. It is usually us. We fail to act in boldness and faith, and so it holds the hand of God back. We are praying for the miracle many times when we should pray for boldness, boldness to act.

Acts 14:9-10 The same heard Paul speak: who stedfastly beholding him, and perceiving that he had faith to be healed,
10 Said with a loud voice, Stand upright on thy feet. And he leaped and walked.

Do you know why Paul could perceive the man had faith to be healed? Paul had already been fasting. He did not need to call for a special time of fasting. He was ready, ready to be used at any time.

2 Tim 4:2 Preach the word; be instant in season, out of season; reprove, rebuke, exhort with all longsuffering and doctrine.

Paul was "instant" at all times. He was ready through prayer and through fasting to operate in the power of God. Did you notice here that Paul did not pray for the lame man? Paul did not need to pray. He needed to believe. The man had faith, so Paul spoke the Word to rise. The miracle happened because of faith. The apostle transmitted faith to the lame man by the preaching of the Word. Paul could do this because of his consistent life of fasting. No doubt Paul was a man of sleepless nights and foodless days. Nights of prayer and days of fasting. There is no easy road to travel to have this kind of faith.

2 Cor 6:5 In stripes, in imprisonments, in tumults, in labours, in watchings, in fastings;
2 Cor 11:27 In weariness and painfulness, in watchings often, in hunger and thirst, in fastings often, in cold and nakedness.

Fasting makes that 6th sense come alive. Coupled with prayer and meditating in the Word of God, fasting desensitizes the five senses and makes one keener to the spirit realm. The seeing, hearing, smelling, feeling, and taste realm is a realm of the flesh, for the natural man to live in. We as born-again believers are to walk and live in the Spirit. God gets glory when working through people that know they can do nothing in themselves. We give Him all the praise.

There is a great supernatural realm that many of us do not know about. Without consistent fasting and prayer, we live in a lower dimension of the Spirit. Answers to prayer are few and miracles are almost nonexistent. With the act of fasting, the gifts of the Spirit open-up, and an open heaven is available to those that want to walk under it. Without fasting, we will be proud, and the gifts cannot flow through us.

Why do we fast? Because we are not happy with the "norm". We want less carnality and more of the things of the Spirit. There is so much that God wants to give. He has more to give than we want to receive. Are you satisfied with the operation of the gifts in your life? If you have the gift of healing, are you satisfied with healing a few headaches and other minor health conditions? How deep does the gift of prophecy work in your life? Do we become satisfied with where we are? Is the idea "going to Heaven enough"? We can bring Heaven to earth with the miraculous. 99.9% of the people will never pay the price to see what the disciples saw. It is so easy to feel satisfied with what we have, and the little growth and a few sick folks being healed. In 1947 Chuck Yeager broke the sound barrier and there was a loud boom. Some have broken through the flesh barrier and they hear a loud boom of miracles, signs, and wonders. When we feel frustration, that is the signal to seek God. Frustration should not be something where we become tormented or where we just live upset with ourselves. It should prompt us to plan a time of consecration.

6 / SECRETS OF SANCTIFING ONESELF

Let us start by looking at King Ahab.

1 Kings 21:25-29 But there was none like unto Ahab, which did sell himself to work wickedness in the sight of the Lord, whom Jezebel his wife stirred up.

26 And he did very abominably in following idols, according to all things as did the Amorites, whom the Lord cast out before the children of Israel.

27 And it came to pass, when Ahab heard those words, that he rent his clothes, and put sackcloth upon his flesh, and fasted, and lay in sackcloth, and went softly.

28 And the word of the Lord came to Elijah the Tishbite, saying,

29 Seest thou how Ahab humbleth himself before me? because he humbleth himself before me, I will not bring the evil in his days: but in his son's days will I bring the evil upon his house.

Here we find the most wicked King that had ever lived. He was very wicked and very evil. There was none like him to do so evilly. He SOLD himself to evil. Is there a man so wicked that lives today? When the judgment was given to him, he ripped his clothes, went down on sackcloth, and went softly. Wow. God took notice of this evil man in his repentance. Did you notice that he fasted? Fasting gets the attention of the Almighty. Even the evilest king that ever lived, sold himself to do evil, and got the attention of God with fasting.

Ps 35:13 But as for me, when they were sick, my clothing was sackcloth: I humbled my soul with fasting; and my prayer returned into mine own bosom.

Ps 69:10 When I wept, and chastened my soul with fasting, that was to my reproach.

Joel 2:12-13 Therefore also now, saith the Lord, turn ye even to me with all your heart, and with fasting,

and with weeping, and with mourning:

13 And rend your heart, and not your garments, and turn unto the Lord your God: for he is gracious and merciful, slow to anger, and of great kindness, and repenteth him of the evil.

Neh 1:3-4 And they said unto me, The remnant that are left of the captivity there in the province are in great affliction and reproach: the wall of Jerusalem also is broken down, and the gates thereof are burned with fire.

4 And it came to pass, when I heard these words, that I sat down and wept, and mourned certain days, and fasted, and prayed before the God of heaven,

Neh 9:1-2 Now in the twenty and fourth day of this month the children of Israel were assembled with fasting, and with sackclothes, and earth upon them.

2 And the seed of Israel separated themselves from all strangers, and

**stood and confessed their sins, and
the iniquities of their fathers.**

When Nehemiah saw the few people that
remained in Jerusalem, the walls broken
down; the gates burned with fire and the
people in captivity, affliction, and reproach,
he went down in sorrow. He and they with
him wept, mourned, and fasted several days.
God heard them, and saw their humility with
fasting, and in time, Jerusalem and the walls
were rebuilt. When your situation looks
impossible, and your life seems to have no
options, fasting, prayer, and humility will get
the attention of the King of Kings.

**Est 4:3 And in every province,
whithersoever the king's
commandment and his decree
came, there was great mourning
among the Jews, and fasting, and
weeping, and wailing; and many lay
in sackcloth and ashes.**

**Est 4:16 Go, gather together all the
Jews that are present in Shushan,
and fast ye for me, and neither eat
nor drink three days, night or day: I
also and my maidens will fast**

likewise; and so will I go in unto the king, which is not according to the law: and if I perish, I perish.

It looks like sure death for God's people. The King has made a proclamation that cannot be reversed. Queen Esther hears of it through her Uncle Mordecai and proclaims a three-day fast. A fast of humility, a fast for mercy. God comes through with a new proclamation that the Jews can defend themselves.

God can make a way out of no way. Can it get so dark that God cannot lighten the situation? I say not. Fasting precedes favor. The king gives her favor. Her fasting caused him to hold out the golden scepter.

Luke 1:37 For with God nothing shall be impossible. In the days of Daniel, a law was made that no one could pray to any God but the king. Daniel broke that law by continuing to pray three times a day with his windows open and as a result was cast into a den of hungry, fierce, man-eating lions. The pagan king being friends with Daniel, humbled himself with fasting and prayed the night.

Dan 6:18-20 Then the king went to his palace, and passed the night fasting: neither were instruments of musick brought before him: and his sleep went from him.

19 Then the king arose very early in the morning, and went in haste unto the den of lions.

20 And when he came to the den, he cried with a lamentable voice unto Daniel: and the king spake and said to Daniel, O Daniel, servant of the living God, is thy God, whom thou servest continually, able to deliver thee from the lions?

Now, God may not have saved Daniel without the fasting of the pagan king, we do not know. The fasting, humility, and tears of the king probably had its part in the divine protection of the great prophet.

Jonah 3:5-10 So the people of Nineveh believed God, and proclaimed a fast, and put on sackcloth, from the greatest of them even to the least of them.

6 For word came unto the king of Nineveh, and he arose from his throne, and he laid his robe from him, and covered him with sackcloth, and sat in ashes.

7 And he caused it to be proclaimed and published through Nineveh by the decree of the king and his nobles, saying, Let neither man nor beast, herd nor flock, taste anything: let them not feed, nor drink water:

8 But let man and beast be covered with sackcloth, and cry mightily unto God: yea, let them turn every one from his evil way, and from the violence that is in their hands.

9 Who can tell if God will turn and repent, and turn away from his fierce anger, that we perish not?

10 And God saw their works, that they turned from their evil way; and God repented of the evil, that he had said that he would do unto them; and he did it not.

Look at this, 120,000 people in one city (right outside of Iraq) repented with fasting. They were evil, sinful, pagan people. God spoke judgment through a rebellious prophet, and they went down with humility. God granted repentance to one of the largest groups of people in one day in the world's history. Who fasted in Nineveh? The king of Nineveh, every man, woman, child, and even the animals had to take part in the fast. Judgment was pending and, proclaimed by a prophet that was not praying and fasting for the deliverance of the people. Yes, humility with fasting will get His attention.

In Bible times the new wives, children of the bride chamber would fast as their new husbands would go off to war. It could take a year just to get there for battle. The new brides would mourn, fast, and almost starve themselves to death. For as long as their husbands were with them, they would rejoice. It was almost an ongoing party with festivities and rejoicing. It was common for those new couples not to part for any reason in the first year. In this passage, Jesus was giving a comparison of the church and himself. When Jesus resurrected and went back to Heaven, the disciples fasted. Fasting is for the church, the saved. It was not until Jesus ascended that the disciples would fast. Going hungry will not convince God or twist His arm into doing a certain thing, but in contrast, it is to afflict our soul and flesh into subjection to God.

Matt 9:14-17 Then came to him the disciples of John, saying, Why do we and the Pharisees fast oft, but thy disciples fast not?
15 And Jesus said unto them, Can the children of the bridechamber mourn, as long as the bridegroom is with them? but the days will come, when the bridegroom shall be taken from them, and then shall they fast.
16 No man putteth a piece of new cloth unto an old garment, for that which is put in to fill it up taketh from the garment, and the rent is made worse.
17 Neither do men put new wine into old bottles: else the bottles break, and the wine runneth out, and the bottles perish: but they put new wine into new bottles, and both are preserved.

1 Sam 7:5-6 And Samuel said, Gather all Israel to Mizpeh, and I will pray for you unto the Lord.

6 And they gathered together to Mizpeh, and drew water, and poured it out before the Lord, and fasted on that day, and said there, We have sinned against the Lord. And Samuel judged the children of Israel in Mizpeh.

We see Israel in this passage in great trouble because of their sin, and they knew it. They fasted, prayed, and asked Samuel the prophet to pray for them and offer a sacrifice on their behalf. He did so, and when the Philistines drew near to battle, the LORD thundered with a great thunder upon them and defeated them that day.

This is just another example of how God can take a person in sin, hear their prayer of repentance, and turn the bad into good, restore them in every way with the blessings of God. In this flesh is a lot of carnality. Without fasting, your prayers could be hindered to some extent. Fasting will replace the carnality with faith. God sent the answer to Daniel, but the answer through the angel did not and could not get through until he pushed back the plate. A lower faith level hinders the answer but, fasting raises the faith level and the answer can get through.

7 / SECRETS OF GOD'S CHOSEN FAST

Here we will examine probably the most informative chapter in the entire Bible on fasting. I will give you a breakdown, verse by verse, and the subjects within the passage. This is a clear cut "do and do not" explanation from God on the subject. If our motive is not right, nothing is right.

Isa 58:1-6 Cry aloud, spare not, lift up thy voice like a trumpet, and shew my people their transgression, and the house of Jacob their sins.

Verse one is the command of God to the prophet about calling out the sin of the people: We live in a day and age where so many are mostly concerned about being politically correct. Generally speaking, if there is sin in the church, they have to figure that out for themselves. Few churches rarely ever call out sin by name. In this passage, the prophet calls out the sin of insincere fasting.

2 Yet they seek me daily, and delight to know my ways, as a nation that

**did righteousness, and forsook not
the ordinance of their God: they ask
of me the ordinances of justice; they
take delight in approaching to God.**

In verse two, God gives his complaint: You
are consistent in prayer, and you seem to
want to know how I do things. The entire
nation acts as a nation of righteousness. A
nation that did not leave my laws and
commands. You ask for the right things and,
you enjoy it; it seems, you love to seek God.

**3 Wherefore have we fasted, say
they, and thou seest not? wherefore
have we afflicted our soul, and thou
takest no knowledge? Behold, in the
day of your fast ye find pleasure,
and exact all your labours.**

The people complain to God in verse three:
We have been fasting, yet there are no
answers. We fast and there is no move of
God. Do you not see us, God? We have
humbled ourselves and you do not pay
attention.

God begins his rebuke in verse three:

Take notice, on your fast you are enjoying life. You find pleasure in everything you do. You do unnecessary shopping, enjoy social media and television. You read non-Christian materials and spend hours chatting with friends. Take note, business owners, supervisors, managers, etc., on your fast day, you put more labor on those under you. You push them and pressure them. You have eased up, but there is no easing up for them.

4 Behold, ye fast for strife and debate, and to smite with the fist of wickedness: ye shall not fast as ye do this day, to make your voice to be heard on high.

God continues his correction in Verse four: Take notice, you go on fasts to win an argument. You fast to put fear on people to control them. You use fasting as a tool of evil to bludgeon and manipulate them that disagree with you. You think I will honor your fast to control someone.

5 Is it such a fast that I have chosen? a day for a man to afflict his soul? is it to bow down his head as a bulrush, and to spread sackcloth and

ashes under him? wilt thou call this a fast, and an acceptable day to the Lord?

God describes the right motives for fasting: Have you fasted the way I have instructed? It is to humble oneself. To cast down the prideful, lofty feelings you have of yourself. You, that are so high you cannot even speak to the poor man. Should you not bow over like the plants in the marsh? Gather the dirty ashes and sprinkle them on your heads. Eliminate the pride and arrogance. Put on your skin, garments made of the course goats' hair. Lay in it, humble yourself.

This is the acceptable fast. The fast I choose for my people.

6 Is not this the fast that I have chosen? to loose the bands of wickedness, to undo the heavy burdens, and to let the oppressed go free, and that ye break every yoke?

Here are the results of a fast, when done God's way: Your sons, daughters, spouses, and others will have chains that fall off. The addiction to drugs, alcoholism and sexual perversion will break. The very heavy concerns, anxieties, and burdens that you carry in your spirit every day will be lifted. You will go free. Take a closer look here. YOU will break every yoke. YOU will cause the chains to fall. YOU will remove all these things as you fast. Your deliverance will automatically happen through the fast I have chosen. I give you authority through my fast to bring deliverance to those you care about. YOU will break the yokes and chains of bondage.

Oh, what a place to meditate. Yes, Isaiah chapter 58 is the place to find the heart of God in fasting. Correct fasting is about purging our lives and cleansing the way we live. Judge yourself by the Word of God. Let fasting assist you in this cleansing process. Remove iniquity and get rid of the items that cause temptation. A clean heart and a clean lifestyle are crucial. What if you have faith to do miracles and heal the sick, but your heart is not right with God? What is more important? Do not let your gift deceive you. If you can heal everyone that passes by but in other areas you are disobedient to God's Word, well your gift has somehow blinded your eyes. All the good you can do does not wipe away your disobedience. Do you feel that your gift will somehow cover God's eyes on the judgment day? Let us humble ourselves with a true Godly fast of humility. Obedience is crucial. Obedience is more important than all the good you can do for people. Obedience is better than sacrifice. One without the other is not sufficient. We need a clean heart AND we need to be used by God. Prayer with fasting is the key to victory, deliverance, and great faith.

Bible fasting is an act of putting oneself upon the altar of God for sacrifice.

Rom 12:1 I beseech you therefore, brethren, by the mercies of God, that ye present your bodies a living sacrifice, holy, acceptable unto God, which is your reasonable service.

The person of prayer and fasting is an intercessor. They stand in the gap and make up the hedge. They are a repairer of the breach.

Isa 59:16 And he saw that there was no man, and wondered that there was no intercessor: therefore his

arm brought salvation unto him; and his righteousness, it sustained him.

Ezek 22:30 And I sought for a man among them, that should make up the hedge, and stand in the gap before me for the land, that I should not destroy it: but I found none.

Let us finish the rest of Isaiah chapter 58. We have seen rebuke, correction, and instruction and now we will see great promises and blessings.

Isa 58:7-14 Is it not to deal thy bread to the hungry, and that thou bring the poor that are cast out to thy house? when thou seest the naked, that thou cover him; and that thou hide not thyself from thine own flesh?

In verse 7 we see instruction but, indirectly to the fast. What does he want from us? He wants positive, loving works.

- Feeding the hungry.

- Giving shelter to the homeless.

- Clothing those that are in need.

- Also helping those of your own family.

8 Then shall thy light break forth as the morning, and thine health shall spring forth speedily: and thy righteousness shall go before thee; the glory of the Lord shall be thy rereward.

Wow, light is symbolic of knowledge. Revelation knowledge will come to you. Also, the light chases away the darkness. Depression will be ushered out by joy. Your health, your wellness will improve. Your body will heal. God will call you righteous and His glory will be your rear protection. He will be on all sides of you as a shield.

9 Then shalt thou call, and the Lord shall answer; thou shalt cry, and he shall say, Here I am. If thou take away from the midst of thee the

yoke, the putting forth of the finger, and speaking vanity;

By doing the correct fast, God's way, you will defeat every bondage and break every chain. God will be there when you call upon Him. He will talk back with you when you talk to Him.

10 And if thou draw out thy soul to the hungry, and satisfy the afflicted soul; then shall thy light rise in obscurity, and thy darkness be as the noonday:
Again, the promise of spiritual light is yours when you help those that are in trouble and temptation and feeding those in need of food.

11 And the Lord shall guide thee continually, and satisfy thy soul in drought, and make fat thy bones: and thou shalt be like a watered garden, and like a spring of water, whose waters fail not.

Yes, fasting will make you sensitive to the Spirit so he can guide and direct your steps in all areas of life. In times of spiritual drought and natural drought, your life will be like a well-watered garden with constant flowing streams. Your blessings will come from all directions.

12 And they that shall be of thee shall build the old waste places: thou shalt raise up the foundations of many generations; and thou shalt be called, The repairer of the breach, The restorer of paths to dwell in.

Because of fasting, you will have a new ministry, an enhanced ministry. You will rebuild the lives of people that have lost everything. You will affect entire families and generations of people.

13 If thou turn away thy foot from the sabbath, from doing thy pleasure on my holy day; and call the sabbath a delight, the holy of the Lord, honourable; and shalt honour him, not doing thine own ways, nor finding thine own pleasure, nor speaking thine own words:

If you keep the Holy Spirit as your rest, which is your sabbath and honor Him in all you do...

14 Then shalt thou delight thyself in the Lord; and I will cause thee to ride upon the high places of the earth, and feed thee with the heritage of Jacob thy father: for the mouth of the Lord hath spoken it.

The Lord will raise you to prominent places. Not always in the natural, but yes, always in the Spirit. The Lord has spoken it and will bring it to pass. Just a side note here about the Jewish fast. It is from 6:00 PM to 6:00 PM. It could start tonight at 6:00 PM and end tomorrow at 6:00 PM. The American one day fast is longer than 24 hours. Let us say that tonight you eat at 8:00 PM and you go to bed. All night long you did not eat. The next day you do not eat, and you go to bed and you do not eat all night long. The next morning you eat breakfast. In this example, which I did for many years, was a fast of two nights and one day. Not realizing it but I was fasting a day and a half or 36 hours. No wonder it seems easier to do the Jewish fast. It is truly one day and one night.

Too many believe they are fasting when enjoying pleasures. They watch television, do unnecessary shopping, surf the internet, hang out with friends, play games, drink their favorite drinks such as soft drinks, coffee, energy drinks, and more. Fasting should be a time of afflicting the soul, prayer, and meditating in the Word of God. These individuals are not fasting, they are dieting. The pure in heart will seek to do the acceptable fast, God's chosen fast.

Fasting with the wrong motive will end with no result. Fasting will not and cannot twist God's arm into doing something. It is also important to note that the Bible, the Word of God, always supersedes a so-called revelation or angel that would bring a different message. Nothing or no one has the authority to speak above the Word of God. If what you are hearing is not agreeing with the Bible, ignore it. We must test every revelation up against God's Word. Because you have been on a 40-day fast, it does not justify a revelation that contradicts what the Bible teaches. The Word of God must be our ultimate authority.

1 John 4:1 Beloved, believe not every spirit, but try the spirits whether they are of God: because

many false prophets are gone out into the world.

8 / SECRETS OF MOSES' VISIONS & REVELATIONS

The noble man Moses spent 40 days fasting without food or water. Matter of fact, he fasted back-to-back fasts of 40 days each. He brought deliverance to millions of Jewish people. They received supernatural protection and sustenance for their forty-year journey. He received the ten commandments by the finger of God and many countless miracles of healings and deliverances. He experienced the burning bush and heard God's audible voice. He came down from the mountain and the skin of his face shown so bright that they had to put a veil over his face so they could look upon him.

Through fasting and prayer, Moses became no doubt the greatest man In the Bible besides the Lord Jesus Christ. There is no bypass, no circumventing of the miraculous. It still takes fasting with prayer. Fasting with prayer raises the faith levels to new heights and new dimensions.

Ex 24:15-18 And Moses went up into the mount, and a cloud covered the mount. 16 And the glory of the Lord abode upon mount Sinai, and the cloud covered it six days: and the seventh day he called unto Moses out of the midst of the cloud. 17 And the sight of the glory of the Lord was like devouring fire on the top of the mount in the eyes of the children of Israel.

18 And Moses went into the midst of the cloud, and gat him up into the mount: and Moses was in the mount forty days and forty nights.

The instruction that Moses received from God on this fast is amazing. The complex detail of the tabernacle, the furniture, and all that was is fascinating. Sizes, colors, wood types, shapes, and more were all revealed in this fast. No doubt Moses saw many visions and revelations. When we read the details in the following chapters, we can understand why he was there 40 days and nights on the mount. He did not have a computer nor an iPad, but we know that God gave him a tablet. Two tablets of stone with amazing downloads, the ten commandments.

Ex 31:18 And he gave unto Moses, when he had made an end of communing with him upon mount Sinai, two tables of testimony, tables of stone, written with the finger of God.

Can you imagine this experience? Forty days on an exclusive fast. No friends, social media, smart devices, phones, nothing. Seeking the face of God. This kind of fast becomes, we see a two-way communication, a dialog back and forth. This kind of sacrifice makes demands. As James said...

James 4:8 Draw nigh to God, and he will draw nigh to you. Cleanse your hands, ye sinners; and purify your hearts, ye double minded.

Did you see that? "written with the finger of God". We cannot even imagine the glory of God he saw. This kind of drawing nigh gets the attention of God. No one has ever spoken face to face with God as Moses, and no one has ever fasted like Moses.

In chapter 32 we see the children begin their rebellion and the worship of a golden image. Moses comes down from the mount and in anger, he smashes the ten commandments into pieces. In Exodus 34:28 we see Moses back on the mountain, but this time God made him write out the ten commandments on stone. This is his second fast of forty days. How many days between the two fasts we do not know, but evidently, they were close together. Here is a verse where Moses tells of that second trip to the top.

Deut 9:18 And I fell down before the Lord, as at the first, forty days and forty nights: I did neither eat bread, nor drink water, because of all your sins which ye sinned, in doing wickedly in the sight of the Lord, to provoke him to anger.

Bible historians attribute the first five books of the Bible to Moses. I can believe that, because when you think about it, who wrote the book of Genesis? Moses was not there in chapter one. I believe that God revealed the creation, the beginning of mankind, the sin in the garden, etc. to Moses there on the mountain during his fast. Look at the following passage.

Ex 33:18-23 And he said, I beseech thee, shew me thy glory.
19 And he said, I will make all my goodness pass before thee, and I will proclaim the name of the Lord before thee; and will be gracious to whom I will be gracious, and will shew mercy on whom I will shew mercy.
20 And he said, Thou canst not see my face: for there shall no man see me, and live.
21 And the Lord said, Behold, there is a place by me, and thou shalt stand upon a rock:
22 And it shall come to pass, while my glory passeth by, that I will put thee in a clift of the rock, and will cover thee with my hand while I pass by:
23 And I will take away mine hand, and thou shalt see my back parts: but my face shall not be seen.

So here we can see an amazing experience with God. The Lord proclaims His name to

Moses; He covers Moses with His hand and passes by and allows Him to see His back parts. Look how the original Hebrew defines the "back parts".

OT:268 roja*'achowr (aw-khore'); or (shortened) 'achor (aw-khore'); from OT:299; the hinder part; hence (adverb) behind, backward; also (as facing north) the West. Strong's Concordance. Look at these two words, "behind", "backward". God is not human though He became a man. God is a Spirit John 4:24. He is an omnipresent Spirit. Using this truth for this passage, could it be that God at this point was revealing, not a physical backside of God as He walked by, but could it be here where Moses was getting a complete revelation of everything behind him? I believe so. I believe that here is where God was revealing to Moses the complete history of the creation of the world.

We must remember here that with our translations of the Bible, we do not have the actual translation from the original writings. No one has the original scrolls from Moses or even the apostle Paul. The writings have been copied many times, and we have to consider the language barrier. They translated it from Hebrew, Greek, etc... Taking the KJV 1611 edition of the Bible, we do not know the spiritual condition of the men that did the translation for King James in 1611. Though I believe the hand of God was in it, we know that certain words could have been translated more accurately. I trust the KJV but with it; I have many Bible helps, such as lexicons. to assist me in my understanding. With all that, I do not believe that Moses saw the physical back of God. How can one see the back of an invisible, omnipresent spirit? I believe he saw a vision or had some revelation of the history of creation, etc. I do not believe he saw a vision of the future as John the Revelator did but saw "backward" or "behind" as the original says. Maybe it is just another way of saying he saw the creation history in revelation.

9 / SECRETS OF GETTING DIVINE DIRECTION

It is so easy to go about our life without seeking God about what we do. So many times, we believers buy cars, homes, invest money, change churches, and do a host of other things without even mentioned in prayer. The things I just mentioned can be life-changing for good or bad, but what about the more spiritual issues? Should we just take for granted that God will lead us just because we are saved? Are we automatically led by the Spirit just because we have been born again? I think not. We that are saved must choose to walk and live in the Spirit. That old flesh nature is still with you. That old sinful, carnal nature is there somewhere ready and willing to lead you in every decision you make. Many have the belief system that everything they do is right in God's eyes and that God will lead them and direct them regardless of what it is. Listed below are a few scriptures that refer to doing the will of God.

Eph 5:17 Wherefore be ye not unwise, but understanding what the will of the Lord is.

Acts 21:14 And when he would not be persuaded, we ceased, saying, The will of the Lord be done.

Rom 12:2 And be not conformed to this world: but be ye transformed by the renewing of your mind, that ye may prove what is that good, and acceptable, and perfect, will of God.

James 4:14-15 Whereas ye know not what shall be on the morrow. For what is your life? It is even a vapour, that appeareth for a little time, and then vanisheth away.
15 For that ye ought to say, If the Lord will, we shall live, and do this, or that.

My point is not to say that we need to fast a special fast for everything we do, but in our daily devotions of prayer and in our regular times of fasting, we should bring our lifestyle and life decisions unto the Lord for direction. We may have more serious decisions to make and want a very definite word from the Lord. When that is the case, yes, a special time of fasting could be taken advantage of.

Ezra 8:21 Then I proclaimed a fast there, at the river of Ahava, that we might afflict ourselves before our God, to seek of him a right way for us, and for our little ones, and for all our substance.

Here we see in Ezra how they took advantage of a special time of fasting, so they and their families would have the blessing of God. I typically pray about every vehicle I consider purchasing. There has been more than once I did not pray or prayed a little about the purchase and got myself in trouble. Engine problems and the like soon after the purchase told me I did not pray as I should have. Believe me, when that happened in the past, I was examining my time of prayer about that car.

Acts 13:2-4 As they ministered to the Lord, and fasted, the Holy Ghost said, Separate me Barnabas and Saul for the work whereunto I have called them.

3 And when they had fasted and prayed, and laid their hands on them, they sent them away.
4 So they, being sent forth by the Holy Ghost, departed unto Seleucia; and from thence they sailed to Cyprus.

So, we see here in Acts chapter 13, that the Apostles took advantage of fasting in this important ministry decision. It is so easy to examine a situation. Everything looks perfect and everyone looks right for the position, but God sees what we do not. Remember that He sees the end from the beginning and His thoughts are not our thoughts. Prayer with fasting is such a crucial and important tool for major decisions.

I know of a missionary that felt led to plant churches in a foreign country and his district leaders would not approve it. He kept feeling the will of God in that country and went to the district leaders and they again, would not approve it. He honored their decision and was obedient. Some time went by and his employer assigned him a job position to a certain foreign country. Guess where they sent him? At no cost to him, and with no fundraisers needed, they sent him to that country where he felt led. So, for months at a time, he lived in that country where he was feeling the Lord calling him to and his employer paid all expenses.

He made another appeal to his district leaders, and they approved him for the ministry in that country. So, let us give credit to the minister feeling a calling to a certain country and let us also give credit to the district leaders for saying "no". They probably did not know why they did not feel the timing was right, but because they "postponed" his approval. God set it up with all expenses paid. He could now do the work of the ministry in his off-hours and weekends. Prayer and fasting for ministry are vital for the greatest results.

Acts 14:23 And when they had ordained them elders in every church, and had prayed with fasting, they commended them to the Lord, on whom they believed.

Here is another perfect example of special times of prayer and fasting for ministry. For us ministers, we know that effectiveness in ministry is vital. Money and laborers are not always easily available, but the marvelous news is, by knowing and following the direction of the Holy Spirit, we can optimize every work for God that He leads us into.

10 / SECRETS OF THE ONE DAY FAST, THREE DAY FAST AND, THE "SPIRIT" OF FASTING

Fasting Until the Sun Goes Down

Judg 20:26 Then all the children of Israel, and all the people, went up, and came unto the house of God, and wept, and sat there before the Lord, and fasted that day until even, and offered burnt offerings and peace offerings before the Lord.

We see here a powerful passage about how a short fast (morning until the sun goes down) when done with sincerity, can be highly effective. In verse 18, Israel went to the house of God to seek counsel but did not fast. They went into battle and lost thousands. In verse 21, we see that they went up again to the house of God, wept, and fasted until evening. They again went out to battle, but this time it was different. God gave them victory in battle, and they came home victorious. Sometimes it is more than just going hungry. There must be a logical purpose in the fast. Even though the fast was until evening, it had a purpose. A fast for deliverance, a fast for victory. How many times do we fast until evening or for 24 hours with no purpose? Sure, there is a fast for discipline when maybe there is no set purpose but only to keep the flesh under subjection. How many times are we up against a sickness, a diagnosis, or other major life setback and we do not with purpose, fast specifically and pin pointedly at that problem? If we will, God will step in and smite our enemies.

Let me point out here, this was not a normal day to give up food until evening. They were not finishing up shopping at Walmart, picking up the dry cleaning, and running errands. They went to the house of God, they wept, sat before the Lord (waited to hear from God) with fasting. This is different than you can see compared to the fast we are used to doing. We go without food and pray a little if we get the time and then move about our day. The people of Israel were serious about this battle, they had a deadline. We have deadlines too, but we let come what will and accept the outcome as the will of God. The outcome we receive may have not at all been the will of God. It is easy to accept the bad as the will of God. We need to do like Israel and get dissatisfied and go back to the house of God, this time with weeping and fasting. Listen, God never stumbles over an intercessor! He will take notice.

Judg 20:35 And the Lord smote Benjamin before Israel: and the children of Israel destroyed of the Benjamites that day twenty and five thousand and an hundred men: all these drew the sword.

There we go, the victory that God gives. God smote the enemy for Israel. God can smite that cancer. God can smite the jobless situation. God can smite that family split. It does not matter what it is, God can do it. If you will just do the insignificant thing, God will do the gigantic thing. If you will fast with clear directives, God will step in with a miracle that will blow your mind.

Angel Food Cake

1 Kings 19:4-13 But he himself went a day's journey into the wilderness, and came and sat down under a juniper tree: and he requested for himself that he might die; and said, It is enough; now, O Lord, take away my life; for I am not better than my fathers.

5 And as he lay and slept under a juniper tree, behold, then an angel touched him, and said unto him, Arise and eat.

6 And he looked, and, behold, there was a cake baken on the coals, and a cruse of water at his head. And he did eat and drink, and laid him down again.

7 And the angel of the Lord came again the second time, and touched him, and said, Arise and eat; because the journey is too great for thee.

8 And he arose, and did eat and drink, and went in the strength of that meat forty days and forty nights unto Horeb the mount of God.

9 And he came thither unto a cave, and lodged there; and, behold, the word of the Lord came to him, and

he said unto him, What doest thou here, Elijah?

10 And he said, I have been very jealous for the Lord God of hosts: for the children of Israel have forsaken thy covenant, thrown down thine altars, and slain thy prophets with the sword; and I, even I only, am left; and they seek my life, to take it away.

11 And he said, Go forth, and stand upon the mount before the Lord. And, behold, the Lord passed by, and a great and strong wind rent the mountains, and brake in pieces the rocks before the Lord; but the Lord was not in the wind: and after the wind an earthquake; but the Lord was not in the earthquake:

12 And after the earthquake a fire; but the Lord was not in the fire: and after the fire a still small voice.

13 And it was so, when Elijah heard it, that he wrapped his face in his mantle, and went out, and stood in the entering in of the cave. And, behold, there came a voice unto him, and said, What doest thou here, Elijah?

Here we have the first "angel food cake". Elijah is feeling depressed, discouraged, and sleeping under a tree. An angel awakens him to eat, for the journey is long. He eats and goes back to sleep. The angel awakens him again and says eat. He eats again and began a journey of forty days on the energy of that angel food cake. God miraculously sustained him. After getting to the cave at Horeb, the mountain of God, he began speaking to Elijah. After a bit, there was a great wind that rends and broke the rocks (possible avalanche and or tornado that destroyed a sizeable area) of the mountain. After that, there was an earthquake. Next, there was a fire. Can you imagine a forest fire nearby? God did all of this to test the prophet. Too many of us will get excited with the surrounding commotion of what God is doing. But, wait... there was a still small voice. The prophet hears the voice of the Lord. Do not let the surrounding distractions affect you. If he had not eaten, he would not have made it to Horeb where God would test his sensitivity. Do not wait for God to shake everything around you to get your attention. The act of fasting can make you more able to hear his voice. If you think you hear his voice without fasting, what in the world would you hear from God if you were fasting?

The Three-Day Fast

Let us look at Esther. The book of Esther never mentions God. Though He is everywhere working on the behalf of His people.

Est 4:16 Go, gather together all the Jews that are present in Shushan, and fast ye for me, and neither eat nor drink three days, night or day: I also and my maidens will fast likewise; and so will I go in unto the king, which is not according to the law: and if I perish, I perish.

To make a lengthy story short, Esther was a Jew, God elevated her to the status of Queen. The King himself and most people did not know she was a Jew.

There was a man named Haman that had great detest for the Jews and tricked the King into making a decree that all the Jews would be killed, with no hope of defending themselves. When Queen Esther heard of this plot, she proclaimed a fast among her maidens and all the Jews to join her. She and they fast for three days with no food or water. This was a significant time of mourning and humility before God. They were seeking his grace and divine protection from the upcoming slaughter.

The Queen made a feast for the King and, also Haman. Haman was, can we say, the King's right-hand man. At the feast, Esther revealed the plot of Haman to annihilate the Jews (which would also include herself). When the King learned the details. He had Haman hung until death, and made a decree for the Jews, that they could defend themselves in this upcoming attack. The result was a victory for the Jews. Why? Because one woman in her humility proclaimed a three-day fast which brought a great turnaround in the King for the deliverance of God's people. Does the King of Kings need to turn toward your situation? Does he need to make a proclamation throughout your province? Does it seem that destruction will be your bitter end? Take the attitude of Esther. Proclaim a fast of three days if need be and watch the hand of God work.

Saul Fasts Three Days

The great Saul, killer of Christians, was arresting and sending out warrants for the arrest of Christians everywhere. He was a serious Jew that felt he had a mandate from God to remove the new teachings of Christ from among the Jews. The way he went about it was imprisonment and murder. God wanted Saul's attention, and he got it when he blinded him for three days. Saul prayed and fast with all sincerity during this time.

Have you ever heard of "praying through"? Sometimes we need to "fast through". I believe that is what Saul did here in the book of Acts. He set himself to pray and fast until an answer came. When Ananias showed up, it was three days and nights that Saul was seeking God with fasting. God used Ananias to pray Saul through to the Holy Ghost, and he received his sight again.

Acts 9:9 And he was three days without sight, and neither did eat nor drink.

This man named Saul got a name change to Paul and with that, a calling to be an apostle of Jesus Christ. His mandate to arrest Christians is now to reach the unknown world with the same gospel he was fighting against. Paul was possibly the greatest apostle in that era, or maybe ever, with an unknown number of church plants. He was teaching, training, and writing more of the New Testament than anyone.

Why did Saul fast? As an Old Testament Jew, he knew the power of fasting and how it can get the attention of God. Saul believed that in that present crisis in his life, he needed definite answers. He knew there was a possible doctrinal shift that he may need to take, and he wanted truth at all costs. His current religious convictions and beliefs meant little at this point because of his desperation. He wanted whatever God had for him, regardless of what it was. He knew, with this doctrinal shift before him, his life would now be at stake and a bounty on his head. There was no time to just think about this or casually pray about it. Blind with nowhere to go, food and drink was not an option. He had an extreme situation, and he had to take extreme measures. Without receiving the truth of Jesus Christ, he may have been blind for life. He had no guarantee of anything but stepped out to do what he knew, fast and pray until the answer came.

Yes, an Apostle was born in Acts chapter nine because of a three-day fast. The light on the road to Damascus blinded Saul and with that, he sought the face of Jehovah. He had a fresh revelation that came to him. Jehovah spoke to him when he asked, "who art thou Lord?" The God of the Old Testament that he knew as Jehovah, spoke back to him, and said, "I am Jesus".

Anna and Simeon

Anna and Simeon saw the Christ child because of their fasting and prayer. What a miracle. We do not know for sure, but no doubt they spent decades in the temple and their petition was to see the Christ before they died. Their fasting and prayer kept them alive until Jesus Christ was born.

Luke 2:25-30 And, behold, there was a man in Jerusalem, whose name was Simeon; and the same man was just and devout, waiting for the

consolation of Israel: and the Holy Ghost was upon him.

26 And it was revealed unto him by the Holy Ghost, that he should not see death, before he had seen the Lord's Christ.

27 And he came by the Spirit into the temple: and when the parents brought in the child Jesus, to do for him after the custom of the law,

28 Then took he him up in his arms, and blessed God, and said,

29 Lord, now lettest thou thy servant depart in peace, according to thy word:

30 For mine eyes have seen thy salvation,

Luke 2:36-38 And there was one Anna, a prophetess, the daughter of Phanuel, of the tribe of Aser: she was of a great age, and had lived with an husband seven years from her virginity;

37 And she was a widow of about fourscore and four years, which departed not from the temple, but served God with fastings and prayers night and day.

38 And she coming in that instant gave thanks likewise unto the Lord, and spake of him to all them that looked for redemption in Jerusalem.

Here is a beautiful story of a multitude following Jesus and having nothing to eat for three days.

Mark 8:1-9 In those days the multitude being very great, and having nothing to eat, Jesus called his disciples unto him, and saith unto them,
2 I have compassion on the multitude, because they have now been with me three days, and have nothing to eat:
3 And if I send them away fasting to their own houses, they will faint by the way: for divers of them came from far.
4 And his disciples answered him, From whence can a man satisfy these men with bread here in the wilderness?
5 And he asked them, How many loaves have ye? And they said, Seven.

6 And he commanded the people to sit down on the ground: and he took the seven loaves, and gave thanks, and brake, and gave to his disciples to set before them; and they did set them before the people.

7 And they had a few small fishes: and he blessed, and commanded to set them also before them.

8 So they did eat, and were filled: and they took up of the broken meat that was left seven baskets.

9 And they that had eaten were about four thousand: and he sent them away.

This is a natural example of where the multitude may or may not have been willfully fasting. The fact bares out that they were following Jesus. They believed in Him and wanted to be with Him. They will go without, just to follow Him. In the Spirit, God sees your real hunger. He sees your fasting and will not let your "hunger" go without being met. Your fast is not a waste of time. It will not go unnoticed by the Master.

Matt 5:6 Blessed are they which do hunger and thirst after

righteousness: for they shall be filled.

Whether you feel this is referring to spiritual hunger and thirst or from fasting, "you shall be filled".

Acts 27:9-10 Now when much time was spent, and when sailing was now dangerous, because the fast was now already past, Paul admonished them,
10 And said unto them, Sirs, I perceive that this voyage will be with hurt and much damage, not only of the lading and ship but also of our lives.

Acts 27:33-35 And while the day was coming on, Paul besought them all to take meat, saying, This day is the fourteenth day that ye have tarried and continued fasting, having taken nothing.
34 Wherefore I pray you to take some meat: for this is for your health: for there shall not an hair fall from the head of any of you.

35 And when he had thus spoken, he took bread, and gave thanks to God in presence of them all: and when he had broken it, he began to eat.

When reading the following story, we find that these unsaved men with Paul fasted many days, while on the stormy sea. They were fearful for their life. No doubt Paul was the one to convince them to fast. They all did, and God kept them all alive, even though their boat broke in pieces by the storm. Not only did he save them from death, but an angel came to Paul and assured him of deliverance. This was not one of our "maintenance" fasts they were doing. This was a fast of desperation and God was faithful to deliver. Be honest, our "maintenance" fasts are usually about getting to the end of the fast. The fasting done in the Bible was about getting the miracle. It was to see the yoke of bondage destroyed.

Acts 27:23 For there stood by me this night the angel of God, whose I am, and whom I serve...

Fasting must be a means to seek the Lord. Anything, even fasting can become a ritual. It is for some a weekly religious ritual that is done to make themselves feel good.

2 Chron 20:3 And Jehoshaphat feared, and set himself to seek the Lord, and proclaimed a fast throughout all Judah.

Too many believers are fasting as a ritual, just as they did in the days of Jesus. It is a lost weapon in the arsenal of the apostolic believer. We must use this weapon. It brings an invisible blast into the spirit world that changes people, situations, and entire congregations. You read this today because you seek not to be like the Pharisee. You are sincere and want to do this right.

Luke 18:11-12 The Pharisee stood and prayed thus with himself, God, I thank thee, that I am not as other men are, extortioners, unjust, adulterers, or even as this publican. 12 I fast twice in the week, I give tithes of all that I possess.

The Spirit of Fasting

Rom 1:4 And declared to be the Son of God with power, according to the spirit of holiness, by the resurrection from the dead:

"The spirit of" can mean the "rational soul" or a "mental disposition". It does not mean here that there is some "spirit" floating around and his name is holiness. My point being, Christians can and should have the spirit of holiness. He should have a mental disposition about being holy before the Lord. It should be his inner desire. With this concept in mind, here is what we call, "the spirit of fasting". There is also a "spirit of prayer". The spirit of prayer is a desire to pray. A constant desire that looks forward to the next prayer time. When a person has the spirit of prayer, he longs to spend time in prayer to God. When he is ending his prayer, he then thinks of the next time he will pray. When a person has a "spirit of fasting", she plans her next fast. She wants to fast and looks forward again to pushing back the plate. The spirit of fasting and prayer, in my experience, comes when I force myself into these Biblical times of seeking God. The more habitual I become with them, the more likely I have that mindset. I create within me by habit a "mental disposition" to seek the Lord through these spiritual channels.

No doubt Daniel had a spirit of prayer. He prayed three times a day. Even in the face of threat, he kept his practice.

Dan 6:10 Now when Daniel knew that the writing was signed, he went into his house; and his windows being open in his chamber toward Jerusalem, he kneeled upon his knees three times a day, and prayed, and gave thanks before his God, as he did aforetime.

Moses must have had a spirit of fasting. He fasted 40 days and afterward soon began another fast of the same.

Ex 34:28 And he was there with the Lord forty days and forty nights; he did neither eat bread, nor drink water. And he wrote upon the tables the words of the covenant, the ten commandments.

Deut 9:18 And I fell down before the Lord, as at the first, forty days and forty nights: I did neither eat bread, nor drink water, because of all your sins which ye sinned, in doing wickedly in the sight of the Lord, to provoke him to anger.

To gain the spirit of fasting you may have a fight on your hands. If you fasted last week, it will be a little easier to fast this week but if you have been months without fasting, it may be hard to get started. Is it worth the fight past this flesh? Will the headache, the gnawing in your stomach be worth the spirit of fasting? I say yes. Why? Because of the end result. It is not about going without food. It is about freeing the captives, healing the sick, and the breaking of the chains we will see. You can maintain the spirit of fasting after you end the fast. To do this, do not overeat. Eat only for strength. When you overeat, you invite the spirit of gluttony. Your body will easily go into a "cramming" mode if you are not careful. When you allow this, you break the spirit of the fast. The key is "self-control". You can eat but do not let it control you.

Eccl 10:17 Blessed art thou, O land, when thy king is the son of nobles, and thy princes eat in due season, for strength, and not for drunkenness.

The word "drunkenness" here is not referring to alcoholic drunkenness. It is referring to indulgence or a lack of self-control in anything, including eating. Look at "eating for strength". Many of us have a hard time here. We eat until we are full. Eating for strength, helps to keep the "spirit of the fast". You can easily cut your portions, be satisfied and retain the spirit of fasting.

11 / SECRETS OF SUCCESSFUL PRAYING

Prayer is the habit you can do every day and all day. It is that constant communication with God that keeps you at His side. Prayer will keep you sensitive, make you bold and open the channels of the gifts, angels, and even an open Heaven. Coupled with fasting is what I mean. Fasting alone without prayer is almost useless. Prayer is such a powerful force. It moves the hand that moves the universe. Prayer is that daily key that keeps you in tune with God. Prayer is to be a relationship. It is more than something we just do. It is talking to God, communing with God, all day, and every day. By prayer, we learn how God operates, how he moves. We become accustomed to His voice and His prompting.

Rom 8:26-27 Likewise the Spirit also helpeth our infirmities: for we know not what we should pray for as we ought: but the Spirit itself maketh intercession for us with groanings which cannot be uttered.

27 And he that searcheth the hearts knoweth what is the mind of the Spirit, because he maketh intercession for the saints according to the will of God.

Yes, the Spirit makes intercession for us, the church, and anyone in need as he the Spirit calls for. Most of the time we are praying according to what we see and hear. We do not know the underlying spiritual need or even the cause of a particular situation. When we allow the Spirit to pray through us, then the Spirit can answer according to the perfect will of God. In our known tongue we pray according to what we know, but when the Spirit is praying through us, that is what God knows and God knows all things.

1 Thess 5:17 17 Pray without ceasing. KJV

1 Thess 5:17 Never stop praying. NLT

We need a constant spirit of prayer. It is not that we need to be kneeling all the time but there is an inner prayer that can go out all day long. It can be called a "desire", a reaching, desiring for God 24/7. It is where He becomes your longing all the time. It is like when a person falls in love. He may be on the job, shooting baskets in a basketball game or whatever but there is a longing to be with and communicate with that new love.

1 Tim 2:8 I will therefore that men pray every where, lifting up holy hands, without wrath and doubting.

Oh, the desire to pray. Again, you can pray everywhere, under your breath, in your mind, and with people. It is that fellowship with Him. He longs for it. Therefore, He made man for fellowship. He wants you to love Him and desire to be with Him. A choosing of your own. A passion of your own. This is what He loves.

James 5:13 Is any among you afflicted? let him pray. Is any merry? let him sing psalms.
When afflicted, pray more. An affliction can be other things besides a sickness. In Greek, it refers to temptation and problems of life. Do you want to get through it? Pray. Fasting alone will do next to nothing without this daily weapon of prayer. Yes, it is a weapon, and that a powerful one. Prayer moves the

hand that moves the universe. Prayer in a way is a siamese twin with fasting. When you put them together, they are a force like no other. Prayer is powerful, but join it with fasting, and the prayer becomes magnified. The strength of prayer and the force of the prayer becomes so strong with fasting.

1 Tim 2:1-2 I exhort therefore, that, first of all, supplications, prayers, intercessions, and giving of thanks, be made for all men;
2 For kings, and for all that are in authority; that we may lead a quiet and peaceable life in all godliness and honesty.

In this passage, Paul mentions four types of prayer. They are 1. Supplications 2. Prayers 3. Intercessions 4. Giving of thanks. Let me do a brief review for you in case you do not know how to differentiate between the four.

1. Supplication is a prayer in your known tongue that has a very urgent feeling. The feeling you have about a known or unknown situation is demanding and emotional. This is not something you have conjured up, but

most likely the Spirit of the Lord has moved upon you.

2. "Prayers" is also a prayer in your known tongue that is a conversation type approach to God. There is no real urgency but again a dialog and fellowship with God that He so loves. It seems strange that Paul included "prayers" in his grouping of the four types of prayer, but he did not want to exclude this important approach to the Savior.

3. Intercession is probably the most powerful of all four approaches to God. It is where the Spirit prays through you, beginning with tongues and then transitioning into groanings, as Paul wrote about in Romans eight. You do not know what you are saying, but this approach requires the whole person.

4. Giving of thanks is what we would call praise. It is praise, but it is also prayer. There are times and many times where you need to lay aside the "do" list for God and just give Him thanks. That love and those compliments do mean a lot to God. He is a very loving God, and He made you to love Him. Many times, I have spent my entire time in prayer in this mode, just thanking Him for what He has, is, and is doing right now in my life. As you can see, these

approaches in prayer have their very own style and purpose. With all of this, prayer should never be boring. Someone might ask how often and how much they should pray. That depends on your desire. Your desire and conscious need for God will draw you to the prayer room. I believe we as Christians should pray daily. I mean to have a time and place set aside to be with God. Though we may be in the spirit of prayer all day long, there is nothing like a special time to get caught up with Him alone. There is no hard and fast rule of how much time we should pray each day, but many people have the practice of an hour with Jesus. Prayer is the daily key to walking in the Spirit. You need to do nothing to walk in the flesh but to walk and live in the Spirit there will be a dedicated effort.

Gal 5:16-17 This I say then, Walk in the Spirit, and ye shall not fulfil the lust of the flesh.
17 For the flesh lusteth against the Spirit, and the Spirit against the flesh: and these are contrary the one to the other: so that ye cannot do the things that ye would.

Gal 5:25 If we live in the Spirit, let us also walk in the Spirit.

Luke 18:1 And he spake a parable unto them to this end, that men ought always to pray, and not to faint;

Look at "to pray, and not to faint" to faint, does not mean to fall over in an unconscious state. It means to lose heart, to lack courage or to get discouraged. Why did Jesus say that? So many times, it is about waiting. If you pray today, you may get an answer today but it many cases you will be waiting. So, you need to be persistent and faithful while you wait. I want to go through several important pointers to help you in your daily prayers.

1. Keep a repentant heart. Do not allow your spirit to become bitter and angry. If you sin, repent quickly. Do not harbor it. Do not lay down at night without making it right.

2. Do not beg. Begging is a sign of unbelief. No loving father wants his kids begging. Ask and believe. Make your petition clear before the Lord and do it in faith, expecting an

answer. Remind the Lord regularly of your petition. He loves persistence. Resist the urge to be frantic and stressed in prayer. Relax and understand, He hears and cares.

3. Do not use vain repetitions. It is ok to repeat the petition but do not use "fillers" in prayer. Here are a few "fillers" that some people use repetitively, "oh God", "stir Lord", "Move God", "Father God". When every sentence in prayer has a filler, there is a reason for that. Maybe he is trying to have a flow with no hesitation. Maybe they are nervous or do not realize they are even doing it.

4. Understand the promises of the Bible. Too many are praying "if it be thy will" when the Bible is the will, but they have not read the will. When praying for the sick, I do not say "if it be thy will". Because I know what the Bible says about healing, I ask specifically for healing for that individual. God wants us to claim his will. Again, the Bible is his will He left us when He died on the cross. Believe it and claim it.

5. Be specific in your prayers. Too many are praying general type prayers. An example of

a general prayer is "God save somebody today". That is a good prayer, but it requires no faith. Faith moves God, not your prayer. A prayer of faith is "Lord save my son today" or "Jesus heal my spouse of this sickness today". Pinpoint the prayer. Be specific. Do not just ask for a job if you need a job. Tell the Lord what kind of job you want. Do you want to work here in the city as a mechanic or do you want to start a cleaning business? Does he already know what you want? Yes, but he wants the communication. He wants partnership in all you do. Ask and you will receive it.

6. While in your daily time of devotion/prayer, be sure to "get in your closet". Was Jesus being literal when he said that? I do not think so. With all those clothes and coats hanging in there and 34 pairs of shoes and boots that you must compete with? I believe his wisdom is saying, "get to a secluded place. Shut yourself in". Go to your room, shut the door, but let those in charge know what you are doing. Silence the phone. Get off social media. Get it dark or semi-dark. Have your Bible and better yet, a Bible on a smart device, so you can see it in the dark. Turn on some gospel music to

drown out the outside noises that may distract you. All your attention needs to be on Jesus. Not only will you be speaking to him, but he also may speak to you. Pray out loud. You may need to raise your voice a tad when praying. It helps some people to focus a little more.

7. Be consistent in prayer. Make it a daily practice at the same time and the same place if possible. Do not settle for "praying on your way to work". You need "closet time". This is where you are molded and shaped by Him.

8. Start each session of prayer with "giving of thanks". He wants your praise and worship. Give it to him. Boring prayer sessions usually happen because somebody brings "their grocery list" so to speak. They have all the "dos" and "don'ts" for God. That is not the way to start a conversation. What if people out of the blue walked up to you and said, "do this, do that"? We must remember the passage in 1 Tim 2:1 about the "giving of thanks". Also note this passage in Psalms. It tells us how to enter into His presence.

Ps 100:4 Enter into his gates with thanksgiving, and into his courts with praise: be thankful unto him, and bless his name.

OTHER WAYS TO RAISE YOUR FAITH
1. "Praying in the Holy Ghost" Yes, praying in the Holy Ghost is another way to build on your most holy faith. This term "praying in the Holy Ghost" can also be known as "praying in the Spirit", "praying in tongues" and "praying with groanings which cannot be uttered". It truly increases your faith. Yielding yourself to God in this fashion is unique and powerful.

Jude 20 But ye, beloved, building up yourselves on your most holy faith, praying in the Holy Ghost,

2. "Trials" The thing we despise the most is fiery trials. I do not ask for these things but when they come, somewhere in the back of my head I know that my faith in God will grow. From A to B to C. From first grade to second grade, and so on, our faith grows. Trials, fiery Shadrach trials. In the furnace

and out again we live and thrive. He is the fourth man in the fire.

1 Peter 1:7 That the trial of your faith, being much more precious than of gold that perisheth, though it be tried with fire, might be found unto praise and honour and glory at the appearing of Jesus Christ:

3. "Hearing the Word" How does faith come? This one is probably the one we like the best. Faith comes by hearing the Word of God preached. Without too much pain, you can do this every day and get another nugget of faith added to your basket.

Rom 10:17 So then faith cometh by hearing, and hearing by the word of God.

12 / SECRETS OF HEALTH BENEFITS

Ps 109:24 My knees are weak through fasting; and my flesh faileth of fatness.

Yes, you will feel weak in your fasting. Everyone is a little different in how their body works and responds to fasting, but there will be days you can hardly go. If you work a very physical job, you may find some days are difficult. The physical makeup of some people will not allow them to go days without food while working a very physical job. Instead of just giving up and not fasting, you can take some juice. Orange juice has been a help to me. I was on a sales appointment once while fasting. I was taking water only. I did not feel like talking, but that was my job. I wanted to lie down and rest for a while. While in the home of this older lady, I was talking business the best I could, and out of the blue she said, "would you like some orange juice?" I did not hesitate. I said yes, thank you. You know that orange juice hit the spot. It picked me up mentally and physically for a little while. God knew what I needed.

While fasting, you will lose weight. If you fast to lose weight, that is okay if that is the sole purpose of not eating. There are wonderful health benefits in fasting. If you are fasting for "spiritual reasons", and your focus is on losing weight, then maybe your motive is a little off. Sure, for us that are a little or even a lot overweight, we are glad to see some of those pounds and inches go away when we are seeking God with fasting. Listen, the health benefits like losing weight which can get a person off their diabetic medications and other medications is a significant fringe benefit.

The motive in fasting is what this is all about. God sees your motive. I would be wasting my time fasting for a serious situation by focusing on my weight. Fasting is too difficult to do. I fool myself by thinking I will get a certain spiritual breakthrough when my focus is on the size of my gut. Yes, in the back of my mind, I know that fasting has certain health benefits. But again, God knows the motive and I will not cancel out blessings and miracles of a fast for having a wrong attitude.

If you are fasting for health reasons or weight loss, let it be just that. If you are fasting to undo heavy burdens or to see the yoke broken, let it be that. With the right motive, the blessings are yours.

Physical obedience always brings spiritual victory. Many times, in the Old Testament God would speak to one of His prophets to do a certain thing in the flesh and as a result, they gained some victory or deliverance.

Today's Christianity has taken every sickness, infirmity, mental problem, and disease to a pill bottle and or therapy for a remedy. God still heals the sick whether it be a sickness of the mind, soul, or body. Fasting and prayer will still raise the faith level for victory and deliverance, and as I mentioned, the fringe benefits for the physical man.

I included some links to great articles about fasting and health. The subject of this book is NOT about health, but it is encouraging to know that God has a health plan. If we will seek Him as he wants, benefits and blessings come from every direction.

Isa 58:6-8 Is not this the fast that I have chosen? to loose the bands of wickedness, to undo the heavy burdens, and to let the oppressed go free, and that ye break every yoke?
7 Is it not to deal thy bread to the hungry, and that thou bring the poor that are three day
cast out to thy house? when thou seest the naked, that thou cover him; and that thou hide not thyself from thine own flesh?
8 Then shall thy light break forth as the morning, and thine health shall spring forth speedily: and thy righteousness shall go before thee; the glory of the Lord shall be thy rereward.

Look at verse 8, "thine health shall spring forth speedily". Through following the spiritual plan God has provided we have fringe benefits that follow. The apostle Paul wrote, "I would that you would prosper and be in health, even as your soul prospers". God is first concerned with our spiritual health. When that is in line with the Word of God then, all the physical benefits come into fruition. I did not have an intent to write about the physical side of fasting but did want to mention it.

Healthline.com helps us understand how fasting can be beneficial to our health. Below are a few benefits. You may need to check with your health care professional before you fast.

Fasting fromotes Blood Sugar Control by Reducing Insulin Resistance. ... Promotes Better Health by Fighting Inflammation. ... May Enhance Heart Health by Improving Blood Pressure, Triglycerides, and Cholesterol Levels. ... May Boost Brain Function and Prevent Neurodegenerative Disorders.

13 / SECRETS OF END TIME REVIVAL

Joel 1:14 Sanctify ye a fast, call a solemn assembly, gather the elders and all the inhabitants of the land into the house of the Lord your God, and cry unto the Lord,

What should we do?

1. Set aside a special time of fasting

2. Call everyone together

3. Gather the elders and all that will come into the house of the Lord

4. Cry unto the Lord

Joel 2:12-13 Therefore also now, saith the Lord, turn ye even to me with all your heart, and with fasting, and with weeping, and with mourning:
13 And rend your heart, and not your garments, and turn unto the Lord your God: for he is gracious and merciful, slow to anger, and of great

kindness, and repenteth him of the evil.

What should we do?
1. Turn to God with all your heart
2. With fasting
3. With weeping
4. With mourning
5. Tear your heart with violence
6. Turn unto the Lord your God

Joel 2:15-16 Blow the trumpet in Zion, sanctify a fast, call a solemn assembly:
16 Gather the people, sanctify the congregation, assemble the elders, gather the children, and those that suck the breasts: let the bridegroom go forth of his chamber, and the bride out of her closet.

What should we do?
1. Blow the trumpet
2. Set aside a special time for a fast
3. Call a solemn assembly
4. Gather the people
5. Sanctify the congregation
6. Assemble the elders
7. Gather the children and the babies

8. Interrupt the honeymooners and call them to this assembly

Joel 2:28-32 And it shall come to pass afterward, that I will pour out my spirit upon all flesh; and your sons and your daughters shall prophesy, your old men shall dream dreams, your young men shall see visions:

29 And also upon the servants and upon the handmaids in those days will I pour out my spirit.

30 And I will shew wonders in the heavens and in the earth, blood, and fire, and pillars of smoke.

31 The sun shall be turned into darkness, and the moon into blood, before the great and the terrible day of the Lord come.

32 And it shall come to pass, that whosoever shall call on the name of the Lord shall be delivered: for in mount Zion and in Jerusalem shall be deliverance, as the Lord hath said, and in the remnant whom the Lord shall call.

And what will God do?

1. He will pour out the Holy Spirit on all flesh
2. Your sons and daughters will speak prophetic words and utterances
3. The older men will have dreams from God
4. The younger men shall have visions from God
5. Your servants, male and female, will receive the Holy Ghost
6. Wonders in the sky and earth will take place, with fire and smoke
7. The sun will get dark
8. The moon will look like blood
9. There will be deliverance in Zion and Jerusalem

Because of fasting, correct fasting, and prayer, God will do amazing things in this end of time. We will see greater outpourings of God's Spirit, the revelation of His name, and mighty miracles. God has spoken it. Not everyone will take heed to what Joel has prophesied but for those that do, whether it be many or few, they will see mighty revival, in their homes, their servants, employees, co-workers, churches, etc. Mighty deeds will escalate, revival outpouring, and revelation will be amazing.

Dan 11:32 And such as do wickedly against the covenant shall he corrupt by flatteries: but the people that do know their God shall be strong, and do exploits.

Prophecies of end-time revival are throughout the Word of God. The revival began in the upper room with the 120. All of them received the Holy Ghost with speaking in other tongues. They were all baptized that day, totaling 3,000 people. When Peter stood that day and preached, the multitude was convicted in their hearts, and asked, "what should we do"?

Acts 2:37-41 Now when they heard this, they were pricked in their heart, and said unto Peter and to the rest of the apostles, Men, and brethren, what shall we do?
38 Then Peter said unto them, Repent, and be baptized every one of you in the name of Jesus Christ for the remission of sins, and ye shall receive the gift of the Holy Ghost.
39 For the promise is unto you, and to your children, and to all that are

afar off, even as many as the Lord our God shall call.

40 And with many other words did he testify and exhort, saying, Save yourselves from this untoward generation.

41 Then they that gladly received his word were baptized: and the same day there were added unto them about three thousand souls.

The miracles, signs, and wonders will not only be done by "great men of God" but also young people. Your teenagers will prophesy and do mighty deeds through the name of Jesus. God will use anyone that makes themselves available. We live in a glorious time. There is much evil, sin, and wickedness, <u>but it will not stop God</u>.

Rom 5:20 Moreover the law entered, that the offence might abound. But where sin abounded, grace did much more abound:

It may seem that evil will prevail, but Grace will bring victory. Revival will happen <u>in Jesus'</u> name.

More books available by Charles A. Rhodus:

- FASTING SECRETS REVEALED | Breakthrough Fasting
- THE URGENT NEED OF THE HOUR | Revival Praying
- HOW TO HELP SOMEONE RECEIVE THE HOLY GHOST | An In-Depth Guide for Altar Workers
- THE ARGUMENT FOR HOLINESS
- SATAN, DEMONS, & YOU | What Christians Need to Know About Evil Spirits

- A MESSAGE FROM HELL | A Fictitious Plea of a Man in Hell
- FOUR PURPOSES OF TONGUES | The Clearest Explanation of Speaking in Tongues
- GOD IS ONE | Topical Bible
- FAITH – 365 | Maximize Your Faith for Miracles

Do us a huge favor and leave a review on Amazon. (www.amazon.com/author/crhodus)

Subscribe to a very encouraging at www.charlesarhodus.com. It will build your faith and advance you in the Kingdom! After subscribing, request your **FREE** digital e-book! This newsletter will contain special offers and promotions from time to time.

All of his books can be found at: www.amazon.com/author/crhodus

Charles' website is: www.charlesarhodus.com

Be blessed by his podcast entitled, Everything Apostolic. Find it on Spotify, Apple & more!